THE
STEAM
LOCOMOTIVE
SHED

· BRITAIN'S LIFE AND TIMES ·

THE STEAM LOCOMOTIVE SHED

An illustrated tribute

David Hucknall

· RAILWAY HERITAGE ·

from

The NOSTALGIA Collection

First published in August 1998

British Library Cataloguing in Publication Data

A catalogue record for this book is available from the British Library

ISBN 1 85794 107 1

Silver Link Publishing Ltd
The Trundle
Ringstead Road
Great Addington
Kettering
Northants NN14 4BW

Most of the material in this book first appeared in *Classic Steam: On Shed*, published by Silver Link Publishing in December 1993.

Printed and bound in Great Britain

A Silver Link book
from
The NOSTALGIA *Collection*

Frontispiece The atmosphere of the steam locomotive shed is captured superbly in this photograph. Rebuilt 'West Country' Class No 34100 *Appledore* stands inside Salisbury depot prior to departure for her next, and last, duty – the Basingstoke Goods. The date is July 1967 and the sun streams in through the roof vents. Steam rises from the right-hand injector and hisses from an open cylinder cock. *George Harrison*

ACKNOWLEDGEMENTS

It gives me very great pleasure to acknowledge those who have helped in some way in the preparation of this book.

I am particularly grateful to Renate McCarron who typed the manuscript with such accuracy and efficiency, and to Chris Silk who dealt with many of the shed logs. I should also like to express my sincere thanks to Mr Derek Mercer who, as usual, printed my difficult negatives so painstakingly, and to Steve Turnbull, whose assistance with shed logs and shed plans was invaluable.

I should like to express my sincere appreciation to Harry Usmar, Alec Swain, Ken Fairey and Roger Duckworth who gave me permission to include some of their excellent photographs in this work. In this context I have reserved my particular thanks to W. A. C. Smith whose superb photographs have contributed so significantly to this book.

Finally, I must acknowledge my own family for their considerable assistance – my wife Susan, who recast my captions when they were particularly tortured, my daughter Rachel, whose eye for a good photograph is infallible, and my son Philip, who made sure I 'stuck at it'.

CONTENTS

Right The entrance to 64A was off Clockmill Road and led into a passage on the left-hand side of which were glass-fronted, illuminated notice-boards. A driver would spend ten or so minutes checking these to see whether any restrictions had arisen on the route since he had signed for his 'notice'. Other boards gave diagram numbers against which were the numbers of the locomotives picked to work them.

From the end of the passage one could look across the lines to the coal stage and the shed. Behind, the sooted sandstone tenements on London Road loomed. When I knew St Margarets it was a mere shadow of its former self as far as its allocation of locomotives was concerned. It had once had a very large allocation of undistinguished engines, and it is hard

to imagine what working then in the place would have been like. Charles Meacher, who had worked there, wrote, 'It was always a dismal environment but on a Sunday night, when the engines had just been kindled, the cold boilers and black reek made it even more depressing.' *D. J. Hucknall*

Below Roundhouse interior, Swindon. Out of steam, three tank engines face the turntable: '5700' Class pannier tanks

Nos 8779 and 3645 flank '1361' Class No 1364, a Churchward design introduced in 1910 for dock shunting. This locomotive was transferred to Swindon in February 1960 from Plymouth (Laira), and when this photograph was taken was still displaying an 83D shed plate. The '1361ST' was withdrawn in January 1961. No 8779 was withdrawn in February 1962, while No 3645 survived three months longer. *D. J. Hucknall collection*

THE STEAM LOCOMOTIVE SHED

INTRODUCTION

I have only a vague recollection of my first sight of a large engine shed. I cannot remember where or when, apart from the fact that it was very early on a summer Saturday and we were on our annual holiday, travelling from Sheffield to Devon on an overnight train. The shed may have been Bristol Bath Road, seen through the tired eyes of a small boy on a misty morning, but, like a single snap in an album, I can still see a line of green-grey locomotives above brown and silver rails. My parents tell me that everyone in the compartment collected numbers for me. Needless to say, the list was lost.

My first real opportunity to get to grips with engine sheds came in the summer of 1952, when my parents gave me a Rudge bicycle. It was no problem at all to get to Canklow, Grimethorpe, Mexborough and Doncaster. At the time, however, I and my contemporaries were not particularly interested in some of them. Canklow and Mexborough had nothing that we could not see day after day at Parkgate & Rawmarsh or Parkgate & Aldwarke stations. Our abiding passion was for the Heaton 'Pacifics', coming out through the latter station on the Newcastle-Bournemouth trains in the morning and returning in the evening – engines such as *Book Law*, *Dick Turpin* and *Velocity*. We would linger until dusk for a glimpse of the Kingmoor and Corkerhill engines – *Ocean*, *Sanspareil* and *Revenge* – that dashed through on freights between Carlisle and Leicester.

Doncaster was another matter. It attracted us like a magnet but had a reputation for impregnability. We used to sit on the wooden fence and watch the traffic to and from the coaler but there was no question of entering the shed proper. Of equal interest was the 'Plant'. This was surrounded by a high red-brick wall, but we knew a place where you could peer over if you stood on the saddle of your bike and steadied yourself against a handy gas-lamp. This gave us a view through the grimy windows of the paint shop. That shadowy shape, covered in patches of pink primer, was surely *Sir Visto* from Carlisle Canal shed!

Over the years how many casual conversations have unexpectedly revealed a fellow devotee of engine sheds! Wistful reminiscences have disclosed that there was, in fact, an unofficial route into Crewe North shed, over the wall or the fence off Lockitt Street. (The only route I ever used was the official one over the footbridge at the end of the platform.) A respectable professional man sheepishly admitted 'Longsight was the only shed I was ever thrown out of'. I have been reliably informed that, with certain sheds, if you appeared in school cap and blazer and began the conversation with 'Excuse me, Sir,' you would not only be admitted to the shed but also have a guide.

When I went to Edinburgh to work in the 1960s, St Margarets was a relatively short distance from where I was living. The nearness of a shed of such a size and history fired my enthusiasm, especially as I now had a reliable camera and an excellent exposure meter. I would also seize any available opportunity to visit other sheds in Scotland. My first chance to visit Perth depot came in August 1964, when I persuaded my landlady to include me in a party of Church of Scotland ladies on an outing from Leith. I even asked the driver to drop me off and pick me up outside 63A.

The Scottish sheds, even in the mid-1960s, refreshed my jaded English palate. The locomotives were tolerably clean and sometimes appeared fresh from the works at Cowlairs or Inverurie. Happily they were too far away from the growing band of so-called 'enthusiasts' who were appearing in English sheds at this time, armed with tool kits and prepared to remove anything of value from locomotives.

Because my unofficial requests to 'take a few photographs' were never refused, I always tried to take them without interfering with the work of the shed staff. I assumed that they were too busy and that their work was too important to have me pestering them with trivial questions.

To me, everything about a locomotive seemed either extremely hot or extremely cold. The sheer weight and size of the tools needed to maintain or clean the fires were quite daunting. Ashpit work, particularly, must have been absolute drudgery – standing under the locomotive, pulling out lumps of hot clinker through the ashpan for long periods, surrounded by corrosive fumes. I clearly remember one man at 64A who regularly emptied the smokeboxes. His overalls were soaked in sweat. I saw his hand, resting on a standpipe, hard, horny and burned. Some depots had mechanical coalers, but in many, men filled tubs and man-handled them to chutes over the tender. On the whole of the Western Region, for example, only three sheds had mechanical coalers.

As I compiled the photographs for this book, it brought home to me the massive under-investment in the railway system that had taken place over many years. Lack of maintenance during the war was never made good. Facilities and equipment, even at large sheds, deteriorated further and further. Work on steam locomotives, already so dirty and laborious, was made harder by an acute shortage of labour. It remains a lasting tribute to the dedication of the staff over the years that locomotives capable of fulfilling arduous schedules continued to emerge from our steam depots.

THE STEAM LOCOMOTIVE SHED

1.
DISPOSAL

Ash, clinker and smokebox char appeared to cover every square inch of the ground in and around an engine shed. From the cinder path to the boundary fences, it was underfoot and often in heaps. In forgotten or abandoned areas it even provided sustenance for clumps of rosebay willowherb and toadflax. Battered wheelbarrows being filled by stooping men scraping and shovelling by the side of almost buried tracks was a sight repeated throughout our railway system in the days of steam. From Okehampton to Kettering and from Stewarts Lane to St Margarets, men were engaged in a seemingly endless struggle to control it.

Coaling, watering and fire-cleaning were the immediate tasks to be undertaken when a locomotive arrived on shed after duty. Engines could come on to the ash roads with fires so clinkered that it would require hours of back-breaking pushing and heaving with shovel and dart, in front of a fire radiating enough heat to sear the skin. The tools were soon red hot and soft enough to be useless. I recall reading about an 'ROD' on the Western Region that came on to a shed with a fire that took a shift and a half to remove.

Underneath the engine, the dampers would be opened wide and ash would be pushed and pulled from the ashpan with the rake. As it cascaded from the pan, clouds of dust would be whirled by unpredictable draughts and winds through the motion and wheels to cover the poor fire-cleaner.

I remember seeing No 60100 at 64A on the track next to the gulley wreathed in dense clouds of white vapour (probably dilute sulphuric acid if the truth were known). Charles Meacher (in *LNER Footplate Memories*, D. Bradford Barton)

comments, 'It hardly seems possible that human beings could survive in such conditions'. He goes on to describe the well-worn path between the ash lyes at 64A and the pub ('Jock's Lodge') used for regular visits to wash away the fumes.

Some sheds (for example York, Leicester and Crewe) had fairly elaborate ash disposal systems. York had a wet ashpit with grills like a cattle-grid where men could walk while allowing the removed ash and clinker to fall into a water-filled pit below. Others, such as St Margarets, had a pit-side slaking hydrant and dumped ashes were doused under and by the side of the locomotive. Whereas York had a crane with a grab to shift the ashes from the pit, 64A had men with shovels and wagons in the gulley.

Smokebox cleaning was the last of the really unpleasant jobs. Depending on the state of the fire and the nature of the fuel, the amount of ash in the smokebox could vary immensely. Sometimes there were no problems. On other occasions, however, the char would be ready to pour out of the door over the bicycle-clipped trousers and boots of the disposal man, over the buffer beam and on to the track. A fine abrasive material that could find its way into the motion as well as the clothing of the fire-dropper, it had to be dug out and thrown well down-wind of the engine. Afterwards, the door sealing face had to be cleaned, the very heavy smokebox door had to be shut, and the running-plate swept. E. S. Beevor (in *Steam Motive Power Depots*, Ian Allan 1983) says that a fair impression of a shed could be formed from the state of the ashpits. He comments, 'If they were constantly piled up with ashes, then there were not enough shed men or the management was indifferent – or both.'

Above The No 1-type coaling plant dominates this 1965 scene at Kingmoor. On a miserable March day in 1965 a dirty 'Black Five', No 45092, and a neglected 'Clan' 'Pacific', No 72009 (formerly *Clan Stewart*) stand amidst a confusion of oil drums and locomotive kindling.

No 72009 was completed in the spring of 1952 and stationed at Kingmoor, one of five such locomotives. Before the depot received 'Coronation' Class 'Pacifics', one of the duties of the 'Clans' involved working the 9.50 am Euston to Perth forward from Carlisle. In September 1958 No 72009 was tried out on the Clacton line of the Eastern Region. It was hoped that five 'Clans' could be exchanged for five 'Britannias', which would have gone to Holbeck. However, No 72009 was regarded as 'little better than a good B1'.

LMS coaling plants are well-described by Hawkins and Reeve (in *LMS Engine Sheds*, Vol 1 The LNWR). Essentially they contained 300 tons of coal divided between two equal hoppers filled using 20-ton containers loaded from railway wagons using a tippler. Even from a distance fascinating details can be seen – the large pair of counterweights on the front outer wall to balance the containers, the wagon tippler on the lower left-hand side and the pair of chutes with jigger motors, each serving one road.

In operation, coal from the hopper was fed on to an oscillating metal plate and, falling over the edge, fell into a chute and was deflected into the tender. The control hut (strong enough to withstand the impact of large lumps of coal) contained the chute-angle controls and water valves for a sprinkler system to lay the coal dust. *D. J. Hucknall*

Above right This photograph, taken at Lostock Hall shed near Preston, shows two engines – ex-L&YR Aspinall '3F' No 12317 and another 'Austerity' – approaching the 'No 2' coaler, built in 1937. In 1938 the vacuum-operated turntable in the foreground was installed. In the centre and on the right-hand side of the photograph can be seen the gas lamps, with their permanently positioned metal ladders, that lit the yard. The cleanliness of the lamp glass, although essential, is surprising given the general atmosphere around an engine shed. *R. G. Duckworth*

Right Stanier 2-6-0 No 42959 (5B) at Springs Branch depot, Wigan, standing in front of the shed's rather odd-looking coaler on 24 September 1961.

In the course of my trainspotting days on the Midland Region line between Rotherham and Leeds, I suppose I saw just a couple of Stanier's 2-6-0s. This was hardly surprising – they were allocated to sheds such as Crewe (North and South), Aston, Preston and Birkenhead. Introduced in 1933, there were 40 locomotives in the Class. I was very surprised to find that they had a power classification '6P5F' and, nominally, a tractive effort (26,290 lb) that exceeded that of a 'Black Five'. *K. C. H. Fairey*

THE STEAM LOCOMOTIVE SHED

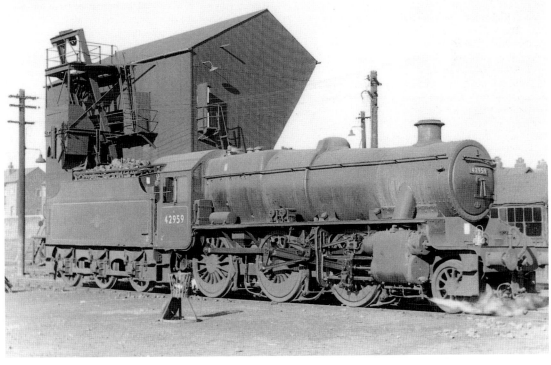

Wellingborough '4F' Class 0-6-0 No 44020 stands under the coaler at Leicester Midland shed (15C) on 3 March 1961. Above the cab of the '4F' the board on the railings reads 'GOODS' – the other road under the coaler is designated 'PASSENGER'. Different grades of coal were available at depots covering both types of duty and the goods engines were given the poorer grades. The running foreman had to keep his eyes open for the driver who tried to top up his locomotive's tender with better coal by nipping under the passenger bunker. To the left-hand side of the '4F', in the road leading to and from the ashpit, stands Staveley '8F' No 48533. *A. Swain*

THE STEAM LOCOMOTIVE SHED

'County' Class 4-6-0 No 1004 *County of Somerset* is seen here by Penzance's coal stage, a typical GWR brick structure with a water tank forming the roof. Inside the stage can be seen a metal mineral wagon containing coal that was discharged on to the metal floor at coaling level and then loaded into tubs. No 1004 was built in 1945. From December 1960 until its withdrawal in September 1962 it was allocated to Penzance mpd. *H. G. Usmar*

THE STEAM LOCOMOTIVE SHED

Left South Blyth shed, Northumberland, on 19 September 1963 – 'J27' No 65876 is being prepared for yet another round of short hauls from pit to port and back. As she stands by the coaling stage one of the crew supervises the watering while the other lubricates the inside gear. Above the locomotive's tender is the coaling chute with tubs containing substantial lumps of coal awaiting discharge. *K. C. H. Fairey*

Below left The disposal crew at St Margaret's set the road for 'A4' Class No 60026 *Miles Beevor* on a drizzly Saturday afternoon in March 1965. Behind the locomotive is the coal bank, where the coalmen filled half-ton tubs by hand and then man-handled them into position over a waiting tender.

By 1965 No 60026 was rather dilapidated, but it had been a King's Cross engine in the heyday of the steam-hauled Anglo-Scottish expresses on the East Coast Main Line and performed with distinction. On 6 November 1956, for example, it was hauling the down 'Talisman', which had left London 23 minutes late. It was driven by Bill Hoole, one of a group of drivers whose exploits were lauded by the railway journals of the 1950s. In a brilliant run not only was the whole loss recovered by Durham, but also arrival in Newcastle was 6 minutes early. *D. J. Hucknall*

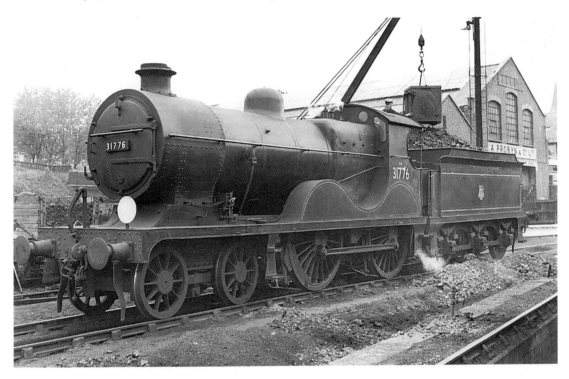

Above At Brighton shed on 23 June 1956 'L' Class 4-4-0 No 31776 is having its 4-ton tender coaled to capacity by a crane-held hopper. The 'L1s' had been designed for the South Eastern & Chatham Railway by H. S. Wainwright and his Chief Draughtsman. When R. E. L. Maunsell joined the SECR as CME, he modified the existing drawings and then had 22 locomotives built – 12 by Beyer Peacock and Co Ltd and 10 by A. Borsig in Berlin; the Borsig engines arrived in England in May 1914. When new the engines were allocated to Bricklayers Arms, Cannon Street, Dover and Hastings. May 1949 found them at Tonbridge, Ashford, Stewarts Lane, Ramsgate and St Leonards. In early 1956 Nos 31776/77 and 78 went to Brighton, working to Tonbridge, Bournemouth and Salisbury. *W. A. C. Smith*

Above Watering the newly arrived locomotive was another disposal task. I photographed 'B1' Class No 61278 at Dundee (Tay Bridge) station on a raw day in March 1965. The sharp silhouette of the typical North British Railway water column shows the small stove strapped to the base to prevent the water freezing in cold weather. As the water is taken on the fireman attends to his varied duties, which would include climbing on the tender to put the 'bag' in position, bringing the coal forward and generally trimming the tender so that everything was secure and no lumps would fall off and cause injury. *D. J. Hucknall*

Right Dominating this photograph is a former Midland Railway swan-neck water column at Canklow shed; behind it, 'B1' Class 4-6-0 No 61394 stands over an ashpit. Scattered on the ground are various tools for fire-cleaning, including long and short shovels. In the lower left-hand corner of the picture and behind the bag of the water column is what appears to be a 'Western Dart', essential a 12-foot long chisel developed on the GWR, which could be used for really badly clinkered grates. In front of the 'Black Five' stands a wagon completely full of ash and clinker awaiting disposal. *D. J. Hucknall*

16   THE STEAM LOCOMOTIVE SHED

DISPOSAL

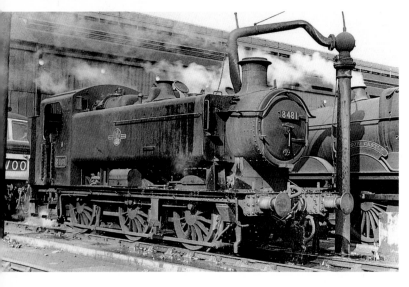

Top Originally there were 40 NBR Class 'D' (LNER Class 'J83') 0-6-0 tank engines, and with the exception of No 8462 the Class was intact on the formation of British Railways. They were very useful engines indeed and, apart from the three shedded at Kipps, all covered at least a million miles each.

Here No 68479 (built by Sharp, Stewart and Co in May 1901) is being watered at Eastfield depot, Glasgow, on 25 August 1958. Eastfield's 'J83s' shunted at Cadder and Maryhill yards and assisted with banking on Cowlairs incline. For this duty No 68479 was fitted with a slip coupling, and the pulley and activating wire can clearly be seen.

The introduction of increasing numbers of diesel shunters brought about the gradual withdrawal of the Class, and No 68479 was one of a group withdrawn in October 1962. The last of the class (No 68477) finally departed two months later. *K. C. H. Fairey*

Middle With sleeves rolled up and jackets abandoned, the crew of '5600' Class 0-6-2T No 6613 prepare to water the locomotive at Neath (Court Sart) shed on 24 June 1958. Water at the depot was pumped from a well fed from the Neath canal and stored in tanks over the coal stage.

Court Sart had two subsheds (Neath N&B and Glyn Neath), and provided locomotives for main-line work, shunting, banking and freight services on the Vale of Neath. In mid-1953 the shed staff included 110 drivers, 105 firemen, 21 cleaners, 38 shed grades, 26 fitters (and fitters' mates) and four boilersmiths and their mates. *K. C. H. Fairey*

Bottom Water spills across '9400' Class No 8481 and tumbles away as her tank is overfilled at Old Oak Common depot (81A) on 8 March 1964. The strengthening sun casts the shadow of the water column sharply across the boiler of 'Castle' Class No 4082 *Windsor Castle*.

No 8481 was a latecomer to 81A, arriving in February 1963 from the Welsh valleys where she had served at Radyr and Barry. By March 1965 Old Oak Common was closed to steam, and No 8481 was withdrawn in June of the same year. *K. C. H. Fairey*

Only a few years before, 'Black Five' No 45118 would have been an extraordinary visitor to Canklow. A clue can be seen in the remnants of the tablet-catching apparatus on the cab side – up until late June 1963, when she went to Newton Heath,

she had been a Carlisle (Kingmoor) engine. Then her only visits to Rotherham would have been on one of the express freight trains such as the Buchanan Street-St Pancras that ran over the North Midland route late in the night. *D. J. Hucknall*

Above One of the disposal crew at Canklow shed is shown clearing char from the smokebox of 'B1' Class 4-6-0 No 61394 on 22 May 1965. This uncomfortable and dirty task was made worse in windy weather, and the noise from the blower jet could be particularly unpleasant. The joint faces had then to be wiped clean and the very heavy smokebox door closed.

Behind the 'B1' is 'Black Five' No 45118 (formerly of 12A and 26A), buffered up to the ever-present wagons full of ash and clinker. Although the crews had no complaints whatsoever about either, boilersmiths apparently preferred the 'B1s' on washout. *D. J. Hucknall*

Above right 'Black Five' No 45461 stands by the ash-lifting plant at Perth shed in 1965. Some of the tools required for fire cleaning can be seen propped up against the tender and lying on the ground. Before the fire could be cleaned, the front and rear compartments of the ashpan had to be cleaned. An ashpan rake was about 15 feet long and the front of the ashpan was dealt with by manhandling the rake through a gap in the firebars and ramming it hard in the direction of the front damper. The rear ashpan could be cleaned using a curved engine rake while standing on the track below the cab. *D. J. Hucknall*

Right Commendably clean, unrebuilt 'Battle of Britain' Class No 34057 (formerly *Biggin Hill*) stands at one of the water columns beside the wooden coaling stage at Salisbury shed. By the side of the rails the debris of dropped fires accumulates. No 34057 has probably completed her very last duty; she was withdrawn two days later in June 1967. *George Harrison*

THE STEAM LOCOMOTIVE SHED

Above Photographed against the background of the repair shop, 'V2' Class 2-6-2 No 60824 stands at St Margarets. The shed was singularly lacking in refinement, and had no ash-handling plant to assist the locomotive disposal crew. In the foreground is one of the ash disposal roads and in the lower left-hand corner a stand-pipe used during fire-cleaning, when red-hot clinker was doused with water. Labouring on the ash-road was hard and unpleasant. Clouds of dust and acrid vapour were produced when the clinker was wetted – the fumes dried the throat, burned the eyes and left a metallic, bitter taste in the mouth. Sweat-soaked overalls and boots lasted half as long as normal under these conditions.

No 60824 (Dec 1937 to Sept 1966; original number 4795) was sent (together with Nos 4796/98) to St Margarets in October 1945 from Doncaster. It is interesting to recall that on 19 September 1955, for the first time on record, an ex-LNER engine (actually No 60824) hauled the 3.30 pm 'Postal' out of Aberdeen. *D. J. Hucknall*

Above right Another view of the fire-cleaning road at St Margarets. Ash and clinker would be ladled out of the firebox by a toiling fireman, the shovel and fire irons getting hotter and hotter the longer the fire took to clear.

Years before, with a line of waiting engines, the process would have illuminated the night as cascades of red-hot debris hit the pit side and the glare from the open firebox lit up the sweating faces of the crews. By the side of the locomotives, piles of clinker would glow, ticking and pinging as it cooled.

These pictures can only hint at the primitive conditions, but a discarded, bent rake, a pile of ash steaming in the drizzle, and rusting mineral wagons already full can still evoke the memory of this laborious and sometimes painful job. *D. J. Hucknall*

Right A schoolboy's view of locomotives at Banbury mpd on the afternoon of 6 August 1958. Looking towards the east across the overgrown sidings and the forgotten piles of clinker, a group of locomotives can be seen behind the elevated road leading to the coaler. In the background is what remains of one of the shed's ash-dropping shelters.

It was obviously the 'Hall', No 4978 *Westwood Hall*, a visitor from Taunton, that had caught my attention, but on either side could be seen a '43XX' Class 2-6-0 and a '2551' Class 0-6-0. At the beginning of her career, in the summer of 1932, No 4978 was a Truro engine, but soon afterwards she moved, eventually finding her way to Taunton. *D. J. Hucknall*

THE STEAM LOCOMOTIVE SHED

2.
TURNTABLES

When a locomotive arrived on shed, the disposal crew were told by the foreman whether or not it should be turned and where it should be stabled. Some sheds had a triangle on which an engine could be turned, but the majority had one or more turntables.

The inconvenience that an out-of-action turntable could cause was immense. In the early spring of 1953, for example, Perth's turntable was replaced. The work took six weeks and during that time some extraordinary manoeuvres were necessary. For instance, the 5A 'Pacific' off the 7.20 pm from Euston travelled to Dundee to turn. Similarly, at the end of May 1956 Penzance's turntable was under repair, and to avoid tender-first working, tender engines were serviced and turned at Truro shed. Several 2-6-2Ts were temporarily drafted to 83F for the workings between Truro and Penzance.

Even by the late 19th century many depots in Britain had been in existence for a very long time. They could be, in some cases, appallingly inefficient. A distorted or corroded turntable, invariably manually operated, could disrupt the work of a depot during breakdowns or after accidents.

During the 1930s companies such as the LMS set in motion ambitious modernisation schemes, which included turntable replacement. The manual turntables were removed, and larger, vacuum-operated machines were installed at over 100 depots. Turntables to the Mundt or Vogele design were in most cases supplied by Cowans Sheldon or Ransome & Rapier. Even this essential work was piecemeal and badly co-ordinated. As Hawkins, Hooper and Reeve (in *British Railways Engine Sheds, London Midland Matters*, Irwell Press 1989) amusingly recall, 'Rather like the successive Gas Board/Electricity Board excavations of our roads, the turntable boys would arrive separately and the roofing firm would turn up months (or years) before or after. . .'.

Even immediately before the end of steam, turntable replacement was thought necessary, some fortunate sheds getting electric systems that were wonderfully easy to control. Elsewhere men struggled to the end, pushing carefully balanced locomotives round hopelessly inadequate 'tables.

In the end, however, it was all for nothing. Diesel locomotives rendered turntables redundant, and this essential feature of steam shed activity rapidly disappeared.

Above 'Hall' No 4935 Ketley Hall, then allocated to Didcot (81E), is seen on the 70-foot turntable at Crewe South (5B) on 15 May 1954. 'Halls' were not a particularly unusual sight at Crewe. In the mid-1950s there were two regular workings of WR tender engines into Crewe station, and one usually involved an 84A 'Hall'. Exeter shed had a regular working through to Crewe on freights in the late 1950s (for example, No 4948 Northwick Hall on 25 October 1958 and No 4944 Middleton Hall on 15 November 1958).

To the rear of the 'Hall' can be seen 5B's coaling plant. According to Hawkins and Reeve, it had been built by the LNWR in 1920 and subsequently modified by the LMS by the incorporation of a wagon hoist. W. A. C. Smith

Above right Perth's 'Black Five' No 45474, coaled to capacity, being turned at Ferryhill shed, Aberdeen, in March 1965. The engine shed at Ferryhill was opened in 1908 by the Caledonian Railway, who shared it with the North British; for years this arrangement was a cause of some friction between the two. Their successors continued to share facilities, although the LNER had a shed at Kittybrewster, on the north side of the city. Gradually, however, locomotives of the former LNER began to predominate, even to the point where, on 29 May 1955, 'V2' Class No 60824 headed the 3.30 pm 'West Coast Postal' from Aberdeen; by December 1956 it was regularly booked to 'V2s'. Ferryhill had a few of its own 'Black Fives', however – at mid-November 1959 it had five (Nos 44703, 44794, 45162, 45167, 45469), and four (all but No 45167) two years later. D. J. Hucknall

What wonderful photographs could have been taken from the flats to the rear of this turntable! Appearing to be almost under their balconies, rebuilt 'West Country' Class No 34018 *Axminster* is turned at Nine Elms on 4 September 1965. No 34018 was one of the Bulleid 'Pacifics' modified according to designs prepared at Brighton under the direction of W. J. A. Sykes (then the CME of the Southern Region), and the result was a handsome, well-proportioned locomotive.

If the locomotive was being prepared for a run it would, after turning, be taken by the preparation crew down to the coaling plant to top up the tender. The relevant headcode would be put up and the engine run forward to await signals to cross the main line and then reverse to Waterloo. *A. Swain*

THE STEAM LOCOMOTIVE SHED

Standing on the outside turntable at Leicester Midland shed on 3 March 1961 is unrebuilt 'Patriot' Class 4-6-0 No 45537 *Private E. Sykes V.C.* (then shedded at Nuneaton, 2B). It had worked the daily pick-up freight from Nuneaton and would be returned in the same way.

The 'Patriots' were introduced in 1933 but were overwhelmed by the large numbers of 'Jubilees' that began to be introduced one year later and gradually they were relegated to fitted freight and stopping passenger trains. In 1950 No 45537 had been one of six 'Patriots' allocated to Preston for working Blackpool expresses. Transferred to Rugby (2A), she was then one of four sisters (Nos 45533/37/41/48)

to be moved on from there to Nuneaton in January 1961. The unrebuilt 'Patriots' were, in my opinion, well-proportioned engines. Occasionally they worked on the Midland main line on expresses between Bradford and St Pancras (for example, No 45520 on 4 January 1956; No 45539 on 19 June 1954). Indeed, the last one of the Class I remember seeing was at Roundwood near Rotherham when No 45511 *Isle of Man*, magnificently clean, was working an up Bradford train.

To the left of the locomotive is a stored '2P' 4-4-0, No 40543. Leicester shed closed to steam on 13 June 1966, but the repair shop containing the wheeldrop, seen behind the '2P', continued to survive into the 1970s. *A. Swain*

THE STEAM LOCOMOTIVE SHED

Left On the turntable inside what had been the Highland Railway's semi-roundhouse at Inverness is Class 'K2/2' 2-6-0 No 61792 of Keith shed. Behind its tender can be seen the impressive stone archway through which locomotives entered the shed; it concealed a 45,000-gallon water tank.

The 'K2/2' Class were unpopular and elderly engines introduced in 1914, but only arriving in the North East of Scotland in 1952-3. Keith's 'K2s' were often relegated to freight work, but when this picture was taken on 25 August 1959, No 61792 was booked to work the 12.45 pm Inverness-Aberdeen passenger train as far as Elgin. *W. A. C. Smith*

Below left The 'K2' Class were long associated with the West Highland Line, a route with formidable gradients. The last working of the Class took placed on 17 June 1961 when, at the request of Mr W. A. C. Smith, 'K2' No 61764 *Loch Arkaig* hauled the 2.50 pm (Saturdays only) Glasgow (Queen Street)-Crianlarich Upper and the 8.10 pm return. Crianlarich lay 8½ miles from Ardlui and was reached by an arduous climb, most at 1 in 60, up Glen Falloch. This photograph, taken at the time, shows *Loch Arkaig* being turned outside the former locomotive shed at Crianlarich. In the shed (which still stands) were a Wickham PW trolley and stored 'D11' Class No 62688 *Ellen Douglas*. *W. A. C. Smith*

Above The tremendous effort required to turn 61 tons of locomotive manually can be seen in this photograph taken at Carstairs mpd on 16 July 1955. The engine had to be set with precision on the turntable, otherwise the effort required would have been too great. Round the edge of the turntable pit is a well-worn wooden track with raised treads to assist the hard-worked railwayman. From 1949 until 1960 Carstairs was coded 64D, then in the latter year it came under the control of Polmadie and was recoded 66E. In the background one of Carstairs's two 'WD' Class 2-10-0s, No 90753, can be seen. *W. A. C. Smith*

3.
SHEDS

The size and shape of the British engine shed was wide indeed, ranging from small, single-road sub-sheds at places such as Helston and Aberfeldy to very large depots such as York, Edge Hill, St Margarets, Newton Heath and Eastfield in their heyday.

The individual type often reflected the history of the shed. The LMS in England acquired some 19th-century roundhouses from the Midland Railway (until the late 1940s Leicester had the original Midland Counties Railway engine roundhouse dating from the mid-1850s). In Scotland the company also inherited sheds from the Caledonian, Highland and Glasgow & South Western concerns.

The LNER's legacy probably dated from the 1860s (St Margarets depot had its origins in the site used by the embryo North British Railway in 1846 to store some engines prior to the opening of the line).

The GWR fared much better. As an early pioneer of standardised designs, it built Churchward straight sheds at Banbury (1908), Penzance (1914) and Aberbeeg (1919), for example, and Churchward turntable sheds at locations such as Old Oak Common (1906, four turntables) and St Philips Marsh (1910, double turntable).

Time, corrosive gases from the engines and general wear and tear wrought havoc with the old sheds, particularly those of the 'north-light' pattern. (The Scottish sheds, usually built to higher standards, seemed to survive better.) Late-19th-century sheds were ridiculously inadequate for 20th-century engines and practice. The LMS and LNER, in particular, began drastic remedial action. The latter

company got off to a flying start and, by the 1930s, had improved its facilities enormously.

The LMS was more studied in its approach, and analysed the situation carefully before launching into the modernisation programme. After a tentative start (Royston and Nuneaton), the LMS became officially committed to modernisation of many of its sheds in May 1933. Over a period of six years more than 40 sheds were reroofed, and coaling and ash plants were installed.

E. S. Beavor (in *Steam Motive Power Depots*, Ian Allan 1983) reports a thwarted modernisation attempt at Trafford Park. Apparently the gas-lit shed was converted to electric lighting by the LMS. Work was only just completed when a Gas Board official appeared with an old contract obliging the railway to take gas for many years. As a result the new fittings were stripped and gas mains replaced.

From an operational point of view roundhouse sheds were better than the straight-through type. They were safer, and a locomotive could be placed on any vacant road. They allowed work on an engine to be carried out in relative comfort, affording more protection from the winter winds that would whistle through straight sheds. Unfortunately, in some cases, as locomotive and turntable size increased, they became cramped and inadequate.

There can be no doubt, however, that in the end British Railways concluded that the roundhouse was the most efficient type of railway shed. But time was running out, and the promise of 1950s projects such as the Crewe North roundhouse was never fulfilled. They were 'altered, curtailed, rethought and cut back' (Hawkins et al, *BR Engine Sheds, London Midland Matters*).

The last shed to be built was at Thornaby. It was opened in June 1958 and could deal with 220 large locomotives. It was planned as a steam shed with two roundhouses, but in light of the Modernisation Plan it was decided that

the cost could not be justified, and one roundhouse was replaced with a straight shed.

The flimsy structures that now serve as service and maintenance areas for diesel locomotives can never have the character, the atmosphere or the tradition of the steam locomotive shed. A large railway shed was a focal point for a whole community.

By 1965 it was a mere shadow of what it had been, but Perth shed always delighted me and I would take any opportunity to visit it. In 1950 138 locomotives were allocated there, the number falling to 97 in 1959. Perth in its heyday was described by G. H. Robin (*Trains Illustrated*, February 1957): 'With so much changing of engines there are plenty of movements to and from the sheds. Stanier 5s from St Rollox, Inverness, Aberdeen and Dundee deal with most workings. . . Aberdeen trains are usually the province of ex-LMS or (BR) Standard types but, at times, Ferryhill shed turns out a "V2" –

even an A2 Pacific on occasions. Most interesting "strangers" are the Pacifics working in from Haymarket and Crewe.'

Here a typical variety of locomotives can be seen, including rebuilt 'Patriot' No 45512 *Bunsen*, 'A4' Class No 60006 *Sir Ralph Wedgwood*, a 'B1' and several 'Black Fives'. The line in the foreground led to the repair shop, whilst the brick building behind housed the shed's offices. Locomotive springs are leaning against the barrier, while the area in front of No 45423 is covered with brake shoes. *D. J. Hucknall*

One of the 'A2' 'Pacifics', designed by A. H. Peppercorn, No 60530 *Sayajirao*, moves past Dundee Tay Bridge mpd (62B) on its way from the coaling stage to the turntable. Only four of Peppercorn's 'A2s' (Nos 60526/33/38/39) were stationed outside Scotland. The rest were allocated to the depots (61B, 62B and 64B) that served the Edinburgh-Aberdeen line. In early 1958 more than 70 steam locomotives were allocated to Tay Bridge, including two 'A2s' (Nos 60527 *Sun Chariot* and 60528 *Tudor Minstrel*) and several 'V2s'. They were used on the through Aberdeen-Edinburgh trains, including the night 'Aberdonian'. From September of that year, however, engine-changing on these services was abolished and every express was worked throughout by either a 61B 'A2' or 'V2' or a Haymarket 4-6-2 of any type. *D. J. Hucknall*

THE STEAM LOCOMOTIVE SHED

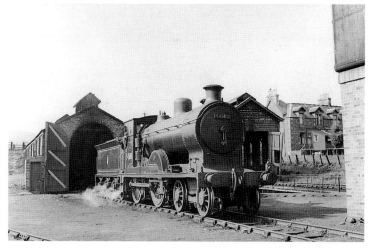

Above Fraserburgh station lay 46⅞ miles from Maud Junction in the very north-east corner of Scotland. In this photograph BR Standard Class '2' 2-6-0 No 78045 (a Kittybrewster engine) is seen at Fraserburgh shed on 21 August 1958; it would later work a freight to Maud.

Three years before this photograph was taken, W. A. A. Bremner (*Trains Illustrated*, October 1955) published an article describing traffic and locomotive working on the Buchan line. He reported that three engines were then usually shedded overnight at Fraserburgh to work passenger trains and freights, and 'almost every possible combination of BR Standard 2-6-4 tanks, B1s, B12s and K2s have appeared on Buchan fish trains'. *W. A. C. Smith*

Above right Crieff had once been significant on the railway map. Until 1951 it lay at the junction of the line from Perth to Lochearnhead and the branch from Gleneagles to Crieff. In November of that year, however, passenger traffic between Perth and Crieff and between Comrie and Balquhidder Junction was withdrawn. In this photograph, taken on 16 July 1956, Pickersgill '3P' 4-4-0 No 54500 stands outside one of the two engine sheds at Crieff, which had been built by the two railway companies associated with the town in the mid-19th century. Neither shed was big enough to accommodate a typical largish engine and tender.

R. D. Stephen, writing of Crieff in LMS days (*Trains Illustrated*, April 1956), said of the shed in the picture: 'In order to align the chimney with the smoke outlet, the tender had to protrude from the back of the shed; and the track was such that it tilted up a steep hill with the buffers buried in a grass bank.' *W. A. C. Smith*

Right Standing outside the sub-shed at Alloa on 5 June 1954 is Class 'J88' shunter No 68346. In the mid-1930s Alloa's two 'J88s' were the responsibility of Stirling shed, but when it became a sub-shed of Dunfermline, Alloa's allocation was also officially transferred.

As the NBR's Class 'F', the 'J88s' were, from their introduction through to the Grouping, that railway's standard light shunter. Their appearance was delightful: their small boilers (maximum outside diameter 3 ft 10 in) was surmounted by a very long, slender chimney. They also had dumb buffers that added to the air of eccentricity in the tradition of the small British tank engine.

The first 'J88' to be scrapped was No 68341, which ran out of control and toppled into Kirkcaldy harbour in November 1954 while dealing with a grossly overweight train on the 1 in 25 branch. No 68346 itself was built at Cowlairs in July 1912. It lasted until October 1962 when it was withdrawn to make way for diesel shunters. *K. C. H. Fairey*

Below In a scene that would have remained unchanged from the beginning of the century, an attractive group of old engines stands at St Boswells on the evening of 12 June 1954. At the platform Worsdell Class 'G5' 0-4-4T No 67268, of Tweedmouth shed, waits to work the 7.15 pm train to Berwick along the Tweedside line, which ran through the belt of rich farmland between the Tweed and the Cheviot Hills and served Roxburgh, Kelso, Cornhill-on-Tweed and Norham. The 'G5s' were built by the North Eastern Railway in the period 1894-1901.

In the yard of the stone-built shed (a sub-shed of Hawick) stand two ex-North British Railway engines, 'J36' Class (built between 1888 and 1901) No 65331 obscuring a Class 'J35' (designed by Reid and introduced 1906-19). *W. A. C. Smith*

Work is in progress at Boat of Garten shed on 'K2' Class 2-6-0 No 61793 and McIntosh '3F' No 57634 as the 9.45 am Inverness to Glasgow/Edinburgh approaches headed by No 45472 on 31 August 1955. Boat of Garten was on a branch radiating from Keith and, from the North, it was approached by what at first appeared to be a double track but was in fact two parallel single tracks. Freight traffic was worked mostly by 'K2s' and 'D40' 4-4-0s. In the '50s Boat of Garten had two freights per day. One, leaving Keith Junction at 12.40 pm, went up to Aviemore, then the locomotive returned to spend the night at Boat of Garten shed in company with a 'D40' which worked the passenger service of three trains to Craigellachie and back. *W. A. C. Smith*

Above The railway shed at Seafield occupied a site between the sea and the Portobello to Leith road. In 1964/65 I would walk past the site regularly, but by then the sidings were invariably deserted although a working water column with a stove heater still stood.

The origins of the shed lay in an incredibly speculative venture whereby the Caledonian Railway had attempted to attract traffic generated by Leith Docks away from the North British Railway. It opened in 1902, but ten years later the CR let the building to the NBR, and it lay derelict until the Second World War when the LNER outstationed freight locomotives there to relieve congestion at 64A.

'Leith Docks shed' was closed in October 1962, but this photograph, taken looking north on 25 August of that year, shows an ex-NBR 'J37' Class No 64599. Also on shed at the time were 'J37s' Nos 64603/5, 'J36' No 65327 and 'J38s' Nos 65922/29. Dumped were 'V2' No 60825, 'V3' Nos 67605/6/49 and 'N15' Nos 69135/50. *W. A. C. Smith*

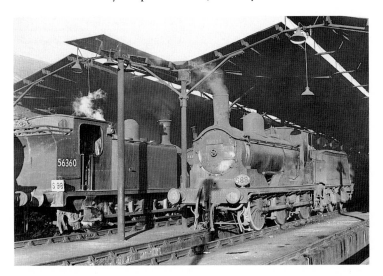

Left Hamilton was a coal-mining district opposite Motherwell on the south bank of the River Clyde, and the Caledonian Railway built a locomotive depot there on a site to the north of Hamilton West station.

In this evening scene on 18 June 1959 the lowering sun illuminates two former Caledonian engines 'on shed' at Hamilton. By any standards the Drummond '2F' 0-6-0 No 57335 is dirty, its front number-plate unreadable. Even the scorch marks on the smokebox door are gradually disappearing under the grime. In marginally better condition, one of the shed's McIntosh '3P' 0-6-0 tank engines, No 56360, faces into the shed, its work for the day completed. *W. A. C. Smith*

Coal up, empties back: by far the most important mineral carried on the Midland route south of Leeds was coal. It was hauled along the Erewash valley to Toton sidings where it was sorted and then re-dispatched to the South. The coal came from the pits along or near the line; within a few miles of the Midland line at Rotherham there were several including Rotherham Main, Treeton Main, Aldwarke, Kilnhurst and New Stubbin collieries. From sorting sidings at Roundwood and Masborough, for example, the trains were pulled by engines from Toton, Westhouses, Canklow, Hasland and Royston sheds.

This coal and other freight originating in the Sheffield area required 9,000 wagons daily. Before the introduction of '9Fs' in the mid-1950s, Fowler '4F' 0-6-0s and Stanier '8F' 2-8-0s provided by various sheds were the mainstay of the mineral traffic; later they were supplemented by 'Austerity' 2-8-0s.

Three types of heavy freight locomotives are seen here standing outside Canklow shed on 12 April 1964. An unidentified '9F' is buffered up to '8F' No 48368 (fitted with a Fowler 3,500-gallon tender), and 'Austerity' 2-8-0

No 90122 completes the line. In the right background work is being carried out in the colliery siding on a small saddle tank.

Canklow shed opened in 1900. It was an austere brick-built structure with two parallel pitched roofs, and locomotive accommodation was in the form of a roundhouse with a 55-foot turntable. The Midland Railway laid great stress on standardisation and, in this photograph, showing the southerly end of the shed, unmistakeably Midland features can be seen. On the left-hand side of the picture is the sandhouse; its chimney was a design that could be seen from Hellifield to Gloucester. In the background is a typical Midland water tank on its brick support.

For as long as I could remember Canklow had never cleaned its locomotives particularly well – as long as the number could be read was all that seemed necessary – but by the 1960s there were just too few staff anyway. By late December 1964 Canklow's establishment consisted of 124 drivers, 40 passed firemen, 56 firemen, 12 passed cleaners and 27 maintenance staff. *D. J. Hucknall*

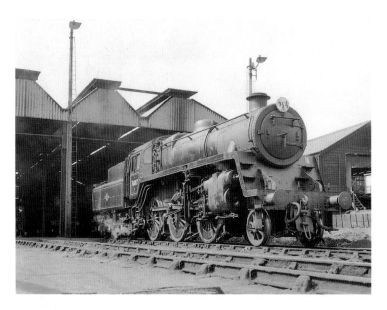

Left When Salisbury shed was opened by the LSWR in 1901, the roof had five pitches covering ten roads. The gable ends were glazed and the smoke vents were separate wooden structures. High maintenance costs caused British Railways to rebuild parts of the roof with asbestos sheeting in the 1950s, particularly the front gable ends. This is clearly seen in this photograph of BR Standard Class '4' 2-4-0 No 76007. Based at Salisbury for several years in the 1960s, No 76007 was the regular engine of Driver 'Alfie' Smith. *George Harrison*

Below The engine shed and yard at Yeovil were often full of locomotives. Constrained by a stream on the south side, the station to the north and a road to the east, however, they were also cramped and awkward to work in. Yeovil's allocation was relatively small, but included ex-SR 2-6-0s that worked mixed traffic trains to Salisbury, Exeter and Portsmouth, as well as engines that came over on the closure of the former Great Western shed at Pen Mill. It was not unusual either to see 'light Pacifics' in and around the shed. In this photograph, taken on 16 May 1964, 'U' Class No 31632, an unidentified ex-GWR tank engine and a 'light Pacific' stand in the yard. Until the late 1940s locos were coaled by men wielding huge shovels. When the crane shown on the left arrived shed life became a little easier, coaling being carried out using half-ton tubs. The crane could also dash around clearing clinker and ash. *K. C. H. Fairey*

Moving from the yard into the shed, here we see an ex-NBR Holmes 'J36' (possibly No 65282), a type introduced in 1888, standing in the deep, dark recesses at St Margarets. The gloom and dilapidation was so typical of structures which had remained virtually unaltered since the beginning of the century. It remains an abiding tribute to the dedication of the shed staff that any serviceable locomotive ever appeared from some of our engine depots. *D. J. Hucknall*

Above A delightful view of the inside of Tweedmouth shed on 12 June 1954 showing Worsdell 'J25' Class No 65727 and Gresley 'J39s' Nos 64941 and 64868. At Tweedmouth the NER branch to Coldstream and thence to Kelso, Roxburgh and St Boswells started. There was also a line to Wooler and eventually to Alnwick and Alnmouth. The 'J39s' were used extensively on the branches together with a couple of 'J72' tanks. In 1955 British Railways began to destroy the Tweedside branch by halving the number of trains and closing stations.

Nevertheless, Tweedmouth shed flourished. At the beginning of December 1959 its allocation included one Ivatt 2-6-0 (No 46476), four 'B1s' (Nos 61025, 61199, 61241, 61322), eight 'K3s' (Nos 61854, 61901/ 17/30/34/52/69/85) and 13 'J39s' (Nos 64711, 64813/ 43/44/68/97, 64916/17/24/25/29/41/49). Compared to straight sheds such as those just encountered, roundhouses always seemed light and airy. Certainly they appeared to resist better the ravages of years of corrosive gases. *W. A. C. Smith*

Below left Because of the huge growth in coal traffic that resulted from the building of the coal staiths at Blyth, it was necessary to have a shed on both sides of the river. The depot at South Blyth was completed in 1879, while North Blyth was opened in 1897 to eliminate excessive locomotive movement, and consisted of a rectangular building containing a central turntable and 22 radiating roads. In this photograph of the interior of North Blyth shed, every engine in sight is a 'J27', that immediately to the right of the entrance being No 65801.

The two sheds, together with that at Percy Main, handled the bulk of the coal traffic in the Blyth area. A typical stint of duty for 'J27' No 65893 in the 1950s from a guard's journal (see J. A. Wells, *The Blyth and Tyne Branch 1874-1989*, Northumberland County Library 1990) would be leaving the shed at 6.15 am, then trips to the collieries at Lynemouth, Bedlington, Choppington and Lynemouth again, with empties. In between, runs from the pits to the staiths were made with loaded wagons. At the end of the crew's shift the 'J27' returned to the shed at 2.40 pm for coal, water and fire cleaning before the next shift took over. *D. J. Hucknall*

THE STEAM LOCOMOTIVE SHED

Neglected and filthy in the gloom of North Blyth, three Ivatt Class '4' 2-6-0 locomotives stand 'dead' on the turntable in July 1967. During its working life, No 43123 had been allocated to Hull Dairycoates and West Hartlepool. No 43050 was shedded at Bradford (Manningham) from April 1960 to April 1967 and may well have been in store at this time, awaiting its final journey to the scrapyard at Hughes Bolckows Ltd in Blyth. *D. J. Hucknall*

Large engine sheds could be cold, dark and slightly menacing. On other occasions they could be transformed by shafts of sunlight into places of enchantment. Here four 'Castle' Class locomotives face one of the turntables in Old Oak Common shed, the silence broken only by a hiss of escaping steam from No 5034 *Corfe Castle* as she comes to rest. No 5087 *Tintern Abbey* and No 5077 *Fairey Battle* stand cold and out of steam. *H. G. Usmar*

THE STEAM LOCOMOTIVE SHED

Tank engines, and particularly pannier tanks, were used extensively by the Great Western throughout its area. In 1948 British Railways acquired 2,436 tank engines from the GWR, of which 1,251 were 0-6-0Ts. Here, in a quiet moment inside one of the roundhouses at Old Oak Common, three tank engines are disposed round the turntable. '57XX' Class No 8768 (an example of an amazingly numerous class, introduced in 1933 and built until 1947), '94XX' Class 2-6-2T (introduced in 1947) No 9423, and '61XX' Class 2-6-2T (introduced in 1931 for passenger workings in the London suburban area) No 6135 typify excellently GWR small locomotive design as they stand side by side. Examples of both the '61XX' and '57XX' Classes are preserved, but the last '94XX' I saw was No 9405 when I was at Paddington station on 23 February 1965. *H. G. Usmar*

Left Sun streams into the motive power depot at Cambridge on 23 April 1962 illuminating one of the sturdy Worsdell 'J15' Class locomotives, No 65469. Built in May 1912 for the Great Eastern Railway, she lasted until August 1962. In true Great Eastern style, she has a stovepipe chimney; the work was carried out at her home shed of Norwich by cutting the top off the standard LNER chimney.

In April 1961 No 65469 had the distinction of being the last steam engine to run on the Wickham Market-Framlingham branch line. *K. C. H. Fairey*

Below This unusual and striking shot shows 'West Country' Class 4-6-2 No 34026 *Yes Tor* at night inside the motive power depot at Salisbury. The photograph was taken using available light and with a long exposure. It indicates how difficult it must have been to work under such conditions and how potentially dangerous the work of our enginemen must have been. *George Harrison*

THE STEAM LOCOMOTIVE SHED

4.
SHED YARDS

The yard of a major steam depot was an unforgettable sight. Close to, one was overwhelmed by the sheer size and power of the locomotive. The bustle of weekday working or the relative calm of a Sunday morning were best appreciated at a distance.

From a well-chosen vantage point, track after track, branching and branching again, leading into the shed buildings, might be seen. There would be rows of engines, some cold, some quietly simmering under a haze of smoke. Here and there, men would be working – standing on the tender trimming the coal, shovelling ash and clinker, operating a turntable – or talking. Occasionally the metallic clanking and the rushing roar and thump from a mechanical coaler fuelling a locomotive would be heard.

Many years after their disappearance, it is easy to recall the sheds – Sundays at Penzance, with row upon row of 'Halls' and 'Granges' standing quietly in the summer sun after

working specials into the town; Kingmoor yard in the mid-1960s, quiet when compared to a few years earlier, yet stacked with 'Britannias' and 'Black Fives', with here and there an 'A3', an 'A4', 'Patriots', 'Standards' – the variety seemed endless.

Today I try to recapture the atmosphere of a working shed at places such as Didcot or Ropley, where the shed yard still remains the focus of purposeful activity. Although the activity is on a smaller scale, the dedication of the men remains as great.

Eastfield shed, Glasgow, was opened by the North British Railway in September 1904. Almost 60 years later, on 12 September 1962, 'B1s' Nos 61396 (65A until January 1963) and 61398 (64A) stand in the yard at the north end of the shed with Class 'J37' No 64623 (65A). The latter's tender is being filled from the water column and already the excess water is cascading on to the track. Behind the locomotives is the 500-ton capacity coaling plant build in the 1930s. To the left of No 61396 is what appears to be the remains of Eastfield's original manual coaling stage. *W. A. C. Smith*

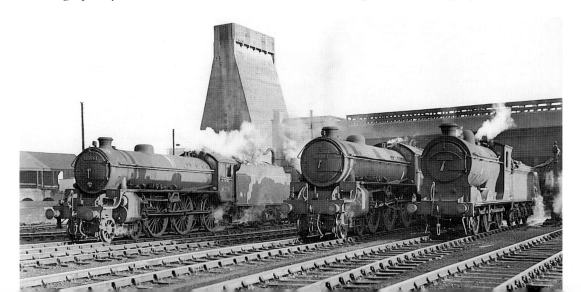

'Britannia' Class 4-6-2 No 70007 *Coeur de Lion* was one of several that were introduced to the Great Eastern section of British Railways in 1951/2. They were highly regarded in East Anglia and, until displaced by diesels, they worked trains between London and Norwich, often covering 500 miles daily on double return trips. Attitudes were different, however, elsewhere, and from Polmadie to Newton Abbot they were accepted unenthusiastically.

In this photograph No 70007 stands, minus its nameplates, in the yard at 63A in the spring of 1965 with 'Black Five' No 45475. The right-hand-side injector of the 'Britannia' is working vigorously and its safety valves are blowing. Dangling through an open window of the cab, the locomotive's 'pep pipe' – used for cleaning the footplate and damping dusty coal – dribbles water on to the ground below. *D. J. Hucknall*

THE STEAM LOCOMOTIVE SHED

Above Smoke from McIntosh '3F' No 57572 covers 'Crab' 2-6-0 No 42879 and 'Black Five' No 45007 at Hurlford (67B) on Saturday 18 April 1964. Approximately 2 miles south of Kilmarnock station, the shed had been erected by the Glasgow & South Western Railway at a point where the main line to Carlisle diverged from the line to Darvel, Dumfries and Annan. In the 1950s and early '60s 67B had over 50 engines; in late October 1961, for example, it boasted 11 '2P' 4-4-0s, six 'Crabs' (Nos 42735/39/43/44/46 and 42880), three '4Fs', seven 'Black Fives' (Nos 45007/10/45124/92/45266/45467/89), seven Drummond '2Fs' and 11 McIntosh '3Fs'. It also had Standard Class '3s' (77015-19).

Although Corkerhill (67A) was the principal mpd for Glasgow (St Enoch) station, Hurlford provided the pilot for the up 'Thames-Clyde Express' as far as Kilmarnock or New Cumnock. The 9.25 am St Enoch-Dumfries was also a 67B turn. Other Hurlford workings involved freight and passenger trains between Kilmarnock and Dumfries, and Kilmarnock and Ayr and Girvan. *W. A. C. Smith*

Below Every engine in sight is an ex-Caledonian Railway locomotive in this view of the yard at the north end of Motherwell shed on 14 May 1955. In the foreground are Pickersgill '3P' Class 4-4-0s Nos 54464/65, behind the former is McIntosh '3F' No 57593 and, behind that, is a Pickersgill '3F' No 57681. Of the two types of '3F', the McIntosh design was the more efficient; the locomotives did a fair amount of passenger work and could be seen frequently on both Edinburgh and Glasgow suburban services. They were also a very common sight on freight trains around Motherwell. No 57681 survived until January 1964 when it was sold for scrap to T. W. Ward at Inverkeithing. It had seen service in many parts of Scotland, having been allocated at various times to Ayr, Hurlford, Ardrossan, Stirling, Carstairs, Wick and, of course, Motherwell. *W. A. C. Smith*

Above A fine array of locomotives stands in the shed yard at Dumfries on 29 October 1955. Visible in this view from the Annan Road overbridge are Fowler '2P' 4-4-0 No 40577 and a sister engine, a '4F' and two 'Crabs'. The 'Crabs', once the mainstay of the Dumfries-Stranraer freight trains, were removed from the depot by July 1964 to be replaced by the ubiquitous 'Black Fives'.

As built by the Glasgow & South Western Railway, Dumfries shed once had a splendid row of many-paned windows where the bricked part of the upper elevation is seen; they were removed in 1947. *W. A. C. Smith*

Above right The pagoda-like tops to the smoke outlets on some of the ex-North British Railway sheds were an inspired embellishment. I saw them first here at Thornton Junction shed (62A) and was completely charmed. Here we see 'D30' 4-4-0 No 62442 *Simon Glover* and 'J37' No 64581 on 18 August 1954. Thornton provided engines for, among other duties, freight workings connected with the Fifeshire coalfield. This shot is absolutely packed with fascinating details – the scorched smokebox of the 'J37', the ashpit guard rails and the complete litter of shovels and fire irons to the side of *Simon Glover* – all rather disreputably bent.

Oddly, many steam depots had sidings with slightly obscure names. 62A had an absolutely fascinating example – it was called 'The Fat Wife'. *W. A. C. Smith*

Right Two locomotives with very different histories stand side-by-side in Perth shed yard on an April evening in 1965. Riddles Class '4' 2-6-4T No 80092 was built at Brighton Works and entered service on 9 October 1954 at Kentish Town. Gresley 'A4' No 60024 *Kingfisher* emerged from the Works at Doncaster and began work at King's Cross on 8 July 1937. No 80092, after hurrying commuters and stock in and out of St Pancras, eventually worked the branch from Killin to Killin Junction in the beautiful surroundings of Loch Tay, while after years of East Coast Main Line express work based at Haymarket (9 May 1939-9 September 1963), No 60024's last stints involved demanding work on the Aberdeen-Glasgow line.

A plaque can be seen on the side of *Kingfisher*. I could never understand at the time why a green diamond should be attached to a locomotive, but I now know that it had once depicted a kingfisher and had been designed and made by Lieutenant A. F. Mortimer RN of Donibristle. It was unveiled at a ceremony at Haymarket on 21 October 1954. I wonder if the official who authorised the obliteration realised that yet another link between the railways and the community had been cut. *D. J. Hucknall*

THE STEAM LOCOMOTIVE SHED

Left A pair of 'V2s' grace the yard at St Margarets, also in the spring of 1965. On the right-hand side, spectre-like, an English Electric Type 4 diesel stands – a harbinger of changes so soon to come. Even by the summer of 1964 the Type 4s were being used increasingly on the Waverley route, and freights to Carlisle from Niddrie and Millerhill, and local work from Portobello to Hawick, all were rapidly succumbing. *D. J. Hucknall*

Below In the period of transition between steam and diesel traction on Britain's railways, there never appeared to be any segregation between the two, although their servicing demands were quite different. In continental Europe, because of the susceptibility of diesel locomotives to the abrasive ash and char generated by steam engines, sheds were usually partitioned. At St Margarets, however, on Saturday 13 March 1965, two 'B1s' and an English Electric Type 4 diesel stand side by side.

'B1' No 61076 was borrowed from 64A by Corkerhill shed in the first week of August 1959 and even appeared at Ardrossan (Montgomery Pier) on an Irish boat train. It was withdrawn in September 1965 and broken up at Faslane in the following November. *D. J. Hucknall*

THE STEAM LOCOMOTIVE SHED

Above In Scotland severe weather can strike locally with unexpected suddenness and it is best to be prepared. For example, on 12 January 1955 the worst blizzard for 25 years struck Caithness and Sutherland. During the night of 16/17 February snowstorms returned, stranding several trains in deep snow at places such as Slochd and Tomatin. Even when spring might be expected further south, snow and ice can appear and, on 21 March 1955 the West Coast Main Line between Lockerbie and Ecclefechan was blocked and seven northbound night expresses had to be diverted via the Waverley route.

Possibly remembering earlier episodes and the terrible winter of 1963, sheds that served lines that could be affected fitted small snowploughs to several of their locomotives. Here, at St Margarets in February 1965, Kingmoor's 'Black Five' No 45138 and St Margarets's own 'J39' No 65929, both Waverley route regulars, occupy adjacent tracks between duties. *D. J. Hucknall*

Right We sometimes forget how short-lived were some of our steam locomotives. 'B1' Class No 61397, receiving attention at St Margarets on 17 April 1965, had been built by the North British Locomotive Co and only entered service in February 1952. It incorporated many features to aid the enginemen, including a self-cleaning smokebox, a rocker grate and hopper ashpan (the flaps at the bottom of which could be opened to disgorge its contents into the ash pit), a Stone's generator and electric lamps (No 61397 has, however, lost the lamps on her central and right-hand brackets). She was withdrawn in June 1965 and was broken up in Faslane three months later. *D. J. Hucknall*

Many locomotives were in an awful external condition in the final days of steam. Typically, Ivatt 2-6-0 No 43084 stands framed by the entrance to North Blyth shed around 1967. Gone are the number-plate and shedplate (possibly removed by bands of so-called 'enthusiasts' who visited sheds with their spanners and pliers prepared to pilfer), replaced by a crudely chalked number. Worthy of comment in the left background is Blyth's north coal staith. These timber structures allowed coal to be loaded on to colliers lying alongside on the river. Trains were propelled to the top of the staiths and wagons brought above loading chutes and discharged into the holds. *D. J. Hucknall*

THE STEAM LOCOMOTIVE SHED

Above A line of 'K1s' at Blyth at 12.57 pm on a summer day in 1966. Peppercorn's 'K1' Class locomotives were built by the North British Locomotive Co, 70 being ordered in 1947. The first batch of 20 was divided equally between Darlington (Nos 62001-10) and Blaydon (Nos 62021-30). A further 20 (Nos 62041-50, 56-65) also went to Darlington. The remainder went to the Eastern Region.

In the 1960s the 'K1s' in the North East took over the colliery duties from withdrawn 'J26s', 'J27s' and 'J39s'. South Blyth mpd was closed to steam on 28 May 1967 whilst the North shed survived until 9 September 1967. *D. J. Hucknall*

Above right On Saturday 24 June 1967, with only three months remaining before the end of steam locomotive operation in the North East of England, the weeds and sand are beginning to encroach on the depot at North Blyth as two 'J27s' stand coaled and waiting for duty. A characteristic British locomotive designed for heavy mineral haulage, the J27s, according to O. S. Nock (*British Railways in Action*, Nelson 1956) were, to the end, 'hard slogging, honest-to-goodness "colliers" and little else'. *D. J. Hucknall*

Right A boy with a box camera captured this shot of the shed yard at Lostock Hall, Preston. Undated, but probably in the period 1948-51, it shows two former Lancashire & Yorkshire Railway locomotives – an 0-8-0 'Coal Engine', No 52916, and an Aspinall '3F' 0-6-0, No 12588 of 23D (Wigan). Lostock Hall shed opened in 1882 and was adjacent to Lostock Hall station, part of the roof of which can be seen in the left-hand background. The station lay between Bamber Bridge and Midge Hall on the Blackburn-Liverpool line. *R. G. Duckworth*

Below Manchester's Newton Heath shed (code 26A from 1935 to September 1963) had been the largest shed of the former Lancashire & Yorkshire Railway system. It had 24 roads and throughout most of its existence had a large allocation of steam locomotives (169 in 1945, 119 in November 1961). During the 1930s the LMS carried out an extensive modernisation programme, including the re-roofing of the northern half of the shed.

In this photograph, taken on 9 September 1959, some fascinating details can be seen, including a relic of L&Y days in the form of the curious water column. The metal stem protruding from its top had once supported a gas lamp, but latterly this had been replaced by an electric light.

The roof, the 1935/36 replacement of the original L&Y hipped roof, is showing marked signs of dilapidation as a result of almost 25 years' exposure to steam and smoke.

The 'Jubilee' Class locomotive, No 45679 *Armada*, was formerly at Millhouses, but moved to Scotland in the autumn of 1952 as part of a very large north-south reshuffle of these locomotives. By this time, however, it had returned south and was allocated to Crewe North. It retained some remainders of its stay – large cab-side numbers and part of the tablet-catching mechanism. *Armada* was to be stationed at 26A from early June 1960. *A. Swain*

Edge Hill depot, Liverpool, must have been stunning for enthusiasts. It was massive – 20 roads – and was the main passenger depot for the area. Its allocation was correspondingly large; in 1959 it consisted of 124 locomotives including 13 'Patriots', 11 'Jubilees', 10 'Royal Scots' and seven 'Princess Royals'.

In this fine study, taken outside the 'old' shed on 24 September 1961, the delightful lines of unrebuilt 'Patriot' No 45533 *Lord Rathmore* are shown to very good effect. Blown by a gently westerly wind, drifting smoke forms an evocative backcloth to the engine. *Lord Rathmore* was withdrawn in September 1962, and scrapped one month later at Crewe Works.

Although by 1961 relegated almost to third-rate duties, the Class had previously been used on very demanding work indeed. As I have mentioned elsewhere, I found them immensely appealing. The first of the class I ever saw was No 45538 *Giggleswick*, hurrying through the station at Parkgate & Rawmarsh in a flurry of steam. From that moment I was forever a fan. *K. C. H. Fairey*

On 2 May 1964 York Minster is barely visible through the murk drifting across the yard. By that year diesel locomotives, particularly the English Electric Type 4s, had begun to predominate and had regular duties to and from York. They were allocated to depots such as Gateshead (52A) and Edge Hill (8A). The former shed was responsible for the 9.30 am Glasgow-King's Cross and some Newcastle-Liverpool services as well as the up and down 'Norseman' between London and York. *D. J. Hucknall*

Saltley's Class '4F' 0-6-0 No 44213 stands by the entrance to an apparently deserted Millhouses shed, Sheffield, on 13 August 1960. Millhouses was opened in 1901 and was the largest of the straight sheds built by the Midland Railway, housing passenger locomotives required for the Sheffield area. Coded 19B in 1935, it retained this identification until February 1958 when it became an Eastern Region depot (41C). At the beginning of December 1959 there were 12 'Jubilees' on its allocation, including No 45590 *Travancore* (the first of the Class I can remember seeing) and No 45609 *Gilbert and Ellice Islands* (apart from No 45637, which was irreparably damaged in 1952 in the Harrow disaster, No 45609 was the first of the Class to be withdrawn). Rebuilt 'Patriots' (Nos 45514/36) and 'Royal Scots' (Nos 46131/47/48/51) also came to Millhouses in early 1960. *W. A. C. Smith*

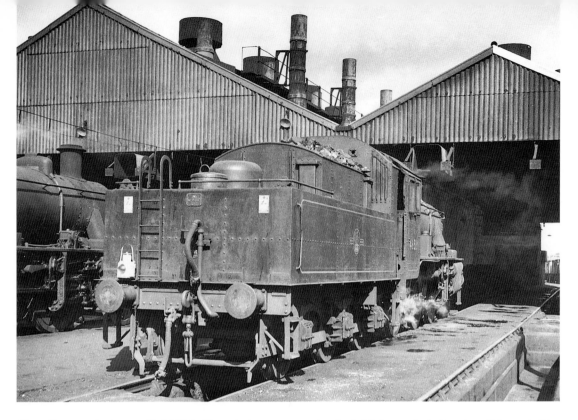

Above Oswestry shed, opened in 1860, had been the largest depot on the Cambrian Railways. The Cambrian must have been a grim old railway – George Behrend, in his delightful book *Gone with Regret*, points out that its directors had been summoned to the Bar of the House of Commons to receive a reprimand for making their employees work continuously for 23 hours a day.

After the Grouping, the Cambrian became the Central Wales division of the Great Western, retaining Oswestry as its headquarters. The GWR improved the depot, initially in 1929 and again in 1939, when the corrugated sheet roof and large cowls were fitted. In 1948, Oswestry's allocation consisted of 36 locos, including two 'Manors' (Nos 7807/8), five '2251s', four '2300' Class 'Dean Goods' engines, six 'Dukedogs' and sundry other locomotives. By 1959 most of the depot's '2251s' had either gone elsewhere or had been scrapped. No 7808 went to Newton Abbot but 7807 had been joined by Nos 7800/01/09/10/19/22 and 27. The predominant locomotive, however, was the Ivatt 2-6-0 of which there were 15, increasing to 22 by the beginning of the '60s.

In this photograph, taken towards the end of the life of the shed (it was closed in January 1965), two of the ubiquitous Ivatt 2-6-0s are standing in the sunshine outside the depot. Incredibly, even in 1992 the external facade of the former Cambrian Railways Works is relatively unaltered from steam days. *D. J. Hucknall collection*

Left Formerly allocated to Newton Abbot before transfer to Old Oak Common, 'Castle' Class 4-6-0 No 5032 *Usk Castle* stands in a siding outside the British Railways-built office block at its home shed. Old Oak's standby engines (frequently 'Castles') usually occupied this or a nearby siding. *H. G. Usmar*

Above Aberystwyth mpd was set at the end of the station in the fork between the line to Machynlleth and the 58-mile long branch line to Carmarthen. It opened in 1864, but when the station was rebuilt in 1925, the GWR improved the shed. Then in 1938 it was demolished and a brick building erected as a replacement.

From 1932 Aberystwyth had been a sub-shed of Machynlleth. In 1948 it had among its allocation of 16 locomotives five '2251s' and six 'Dukedog' 4-4-0s (small hybrids of the 'Bulldog' and 'Duke' Class locomotives). Some 11 years later, on 4 April 1959, '2251' Class 2-6-0 No 2260 (at Aberystwyth even in 1948) and '4300' Class 2-6-0 No 6371 are seen standing outside the shed. The '2251s' hauled freight trains over the Cambrian for many years until replaced in the 1960s by more powerful engines. The '4300s' similarly rumbled along with passenger trains until displaced by the 'Manors' and Standard Class '4' 4-6-0s. *K. C. H. Fairey*

Right '54XX' Class 0-6-0T No 5424 is seen at Banbury shed (84C) on 6 August 1958. Designed by Charles Collett for push-and-pull working, the '54XXs' were introduced in 1931. No 5424 was a relatively long serving member of 84C, having certainly been there in January 1944. She was used on trips such as the Princes Risborough and High Wycombe auto-trains.

Behind the tank engine is the coal stage supporting a 45,000-gallon water tank. To the left, partially dismantled, is one of the shed's ash-dropping shelters; these were erected during the Second World War to prevent the glow from dropped ash being spotted by enemy aircraft. *D. J. Hucknall*

　　　　　　　　　　THE STEAM LOCOMOTIVE SHED

Left With its nameplates covered but in wonderful external condition, Derby 'Jubilee' No 45610 (formerly *Gold Coast*) is seen in the shed yard at Willesden on 12 December 1958. Later that day, in a ceremony at Euston station, No 45610 was renamed *Ghana* by the Ghanaian High Commissioner in London to celebrate that country's independence.

Derby's 'Jubilees' worked to Leeds, Sheffield, Bristol, Bath and St Pancras in complicated diagrams and, as a boy, I would see *Gold Coast*, invariably dirty, regularly passing through Parkgate & Rawmarsh station on some part of such a duty. On 11 April 1955, as *Gold Coast*, it worked the 12.40 pm to Bristol out of Newcastle, the first time since 1949 that a 'Jubilee' had worked a regular service train out of that city. *A. Swain*

Below left 'Coronation' Class 4-6-2 No 46220 *Coronation* at Willesden shed in March 1959. The 'Coronations' (the official LMS name for the Stanier 'Pacifics' that began to emerge from Crewe Works in 1937) worked principally on the West Coast Main Line services from Euston to Glasgow and Perth, and the Birmingham-Glasgow trains north of Crewe. When the English Electric Type 4 diesels arrived on the West Coast in 1959, their days were numbered and, by 1962, the 'Coronations' were seen increasingly on parcels and freight trains. They were regarded by many as perhaps the finest steam locomotives ever to run in Britain. *Coronation* herself was withdrawn in April 1963. *A. Swain*

Above Against a background dominated by the shed's coaler, BR Standard Class '4' 2-6-4T No 80067 (1C, Watford) stands at Willesden depot on 23 April 1959. Willesden, five and a half miles from Euston, provided engines for main-line freight and some passenger trains; it was also a repair depot for Camden, Watford and Bletchley. Noteworthy in the photograph is the large number of tall poles, each carrying two lamps, which would have lit only a very localised area. It is probably very difficult nowadays to appreciate the problems of moving quickly on foot in a shed yard in darkness. *A. Swain*

Below Moving south of the Thames, this is a view of the front of the shed at Nine Elms on 4 September 1965, showing Standard Class '4' 2-6-4T No 80143, Standard Class '5' 4-6-0 No 73115 and Standard Class '4' 2-6-0 No 76053. Dominating the depot is the coaling plant with its concrete hoppers.

Although the last steam run to Waterloo was not to be until 9 July 1967, the feeling of a depot close to the end of its working life is unmistakeable in this photograph. Already weeds are growing beside and between tracks and there is an odd air of stillness where once men and engines would have been bustling. *A. Swain*

Above right 'Jubilee' Class 4-6-0 No 45699 *Galatea* stands over an ashpit at Canton depot, Cardiff. After fire-cleaning, the smokebox will have been emptied of char – in this case, however, the job was incomplete since the buffer beam is covered with spilled char.

Galatea was at this time a Bristol (Barrow Road) engine and, until the summer of 1961, Bristol's 'Jubilees' were the principal motive power for the expresses linking Bristol, Newcastle, Bradford and Kingswear, such as the 'Devonian' and the Bristol-Newcastle and Derby-Bristol mail trains; they usually travelled through to Leeds or Sheffield. With the introduction of BR/Sulzer Type 4 2,500 hp diesels on the Bristol-Derby-Sheffield line, No 45699 and some of her sisters were redundant. In September 1961, *Galatea* (together with *Eire*, *Bengal*, *Shovell*, *Rooke* and *Leander*) was transferred to Shrewsbury. *H. G. Usmar*

Right The smoke from the chimney of 'Britannia' Class 4-6-2 No 70022 *Tornado* can almost be tasted in this shot of locomotives 'on shed' at Cardiff Canton. *Tornado* is standing by an ex-GWR standard 8-inch water crane, while in an adjacent siding stands '9F' Class 2-10-0 No 92231 and, further over, 'Britannia' Class No 70016 *Ariel*. Both of the 'Britannias' were transferred to Carlisle in the late summer of 1961 – *Ariel* went to Canal shed while *Tornado* was moved to Kingmoor.

Clearly shown are the hand holds cut into the smoke deflectors of *Tornado*. These replaced the handrails on the 'Britannias' which had been removed following criticism by the Inspecting Officer after the Milton accident of 22 November 1955. It was concluded that impairment of visibility by the handrails had contributed to the derailment of No 70026 *Polar Star* with loss of life. *H. G. Usmar*

THE STEAM LOCOMOTIVE SHED

Right There were probably few locomotives that would look small in comparison to an 'M7', but members of the ex-LSWR 'B4' Class most certainly did. Here, 'B4' No 30096 and 'M7' No 30375 are shown standing by the coal stack at the north end of Eastleigh shed.

The 'B4s' carried out various duties. One, No 30093, was allocated to Bournemouth for working on Poole quay. No 30096 was one of Eastleigh's engines and, together with No 30102, was the regular yard shunter and station pilot at Winchester City station. One of the pair would remain at Winchester for about a week and then return to Eastleigh for a boiler washout and servicing. Withdrawn in October 1963, No 30096 was sold to Corralls Ltd and worked at Dibles Wharf, Southampton, for a time. *D. J. Hucknall Collection*

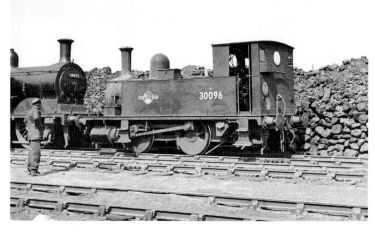

Below Okehampton shed was a small one-road sub-depot of Exmouth Junction. It was made of concrete and erected by the LSWR after the original structure had burned down. No engines were allocated there but it was used for servicing and signing-on. Here 'Battle of Britain' Class 4-6-2 No 34083 *605 Squadron* (allocated to Exmouth Junction) stands in the shed entrance on 4 April 1964. The two-disc headcode was associated with a train travelling between Waterloo or Nine Elms and Plymouth. Okehampton was on the Southern route between Exeter and Plymouth. In the early 1950s there were six through services daily between Waterloo and Plymouth. The fastest time (5½ hours) was achieved by the 'Atlantic Coast Express', which nevertheless took 2 hrs 6 min between Exeter Central and Plymouth (Friary). The final trip of the 'ACE' was on 4 September 1964. *D. J. Hucknall*

THE STEAM LOCOMOTIVE SHED

Bournemouth mpd (71B) was a four-road shed located close to Central Station, and had quite a large allocation of locomotives. In the first week in November 1961, for example, this consisted of eight 'Merchant Navy' Class 'Pacifics', 18 'West Country/Battle of Britain' Class 4-6-2s, two 'N15' Class 4-6-0s, 13 'M7' Class 0-4-4Ts, three Class 'Q' 0-6-0Ts and seven BR Standard Class '4' 2-6-0s. The 'Merchant Navys' were used exclusively on Weymouth and Waterloo diagrams (and balancing local trips to get the locomotives down to Weymouth from the shed and back again). Bournemouth's 'WC/BB' 'Pacifics' could deputise for the 'Merchant Navys', and also worked the 'Pines Express' to Bath over the Somerset & Dorset route. Another turn was the out-and-home trip to Oxford with trains such as the Bournemouth-York.

In this undated view of Bournemouth shed at least three 'West Country' Class locomotives can be seen. The unrebuilt locomotive is No 34008 *Padstow* (rebuilt, however, in mid-1960). To the left is No 34042 *Dorchester* (rebuilt around February 1959). The 'M7' on the right, No 30107, is standing by the locomotive hoist. *H. G. Usmar*

Right Holiday traffic to the 'Cornish Riviera' reached its peak in the late 1950s (see Alan Bennett's *The Great Western Railway in West Cornwall*). On summer Saturdays and Sundays the yard at Penzance shed at Long Rock would be full of locomotives. Rolling-stock would have been stored at Marazion, St Erth and even Gwinear Road, such was the shortage of space at Penzance.

This photograph, taken on 19 July 1959, shows a small section of the yard at 83G, filled with 'Halls' and 'Granges'. It was typical of this period, but thereafter the decline commenced; I returned four years later and things were very different. From left to right are Nos 7921 *Edstone Hall*, 6832 *Brockton Grange*, 7925 *Westol Hall* and 6988 *Swithland Hall*. Also on

shed at the time, and noted down because I had never seen them before, were Nos 4908 (83G), 4913 (81D), 4976 (83D), 6802 (86G), 6824 (83G), 6845 (83G), 6855 (83G), 6863 (83D), 6871 (83D), 6911 (83G), 6913 (83D), 6931 (83E) and 7820 (83D). *D. J. Hucknall*

Below The line between Plymouth and Penzance was difficult for steam locomotives. It had sharp curves, laborious gradients, viaducts and dozens of cuttings and embankments. It was also a line that served the community with branches from Liskeard (for Looe), Bodmin Road (for Bodmin, Wadebridge and Padstow), Lostwithiel (for Fowey), Par (for Newquay), Truro (for Falmouth), Gwinear Road (for The Lizard, Cadgwith and Helston) and St Erth (for St Ives). As late as the 1950s regular pick-up trains ambled along the line, calling at all stations, collecting and delivering wagons.

'Prairie' tanks will always be synonymous with the Cornish branches and, on a Sunday afternoon in July 1959, Nos 4566 and 4564 stand at Penzance shed for servicing. I remember No 4566 as a regular on the Helston-Gwinear Road branch; it was also, almost exactly one year later, the last steam locomotive to be overhauled at Newton Abbot works. *D. J. Hucknall*

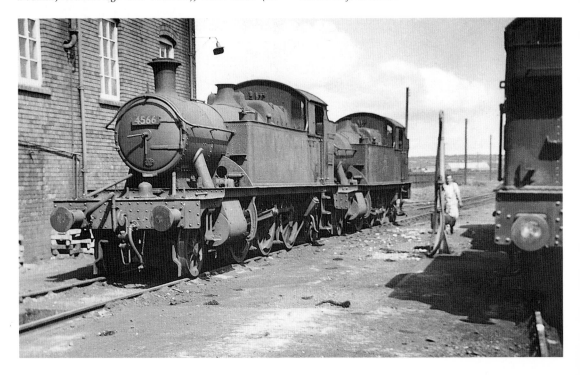

5.
PORTRAITS

Of course, it was always a stirring sight to see an express approaching, worked with full regulator and short cut-off with the driver concentrating on the road ahead, but for me the uniqueness and beauty of the steam locomotive could only be appreciated at close quarters.

It really was amazing that in a class of supposedly identical locomotives, each appeared to have its own character and idiosyncrasies. To read the experiences of men closely associated with engines and their running is to appreciate much more the enthusiasm that they had for their machines and the teamwork required to get the best out of them. Over the years, pen-portraits by railwaymen themselves revealed the 'character' of the steam locomotive; 'Toram Beg' (Norman McKillop), '45671' and Harold Gasson have written informatively and evocatively about their experiences.

'45671' (in *Trains Illustrated*, January 1958) on

'Black Fives' said 'That was a beautiful engine, No 45253. There was nothing that she could not do. . .', and 'All went well until a new batch of Class 5s, built in Horwich, were sent to Scotland and numbers 4796 and 4797 went to Perth. Right from the start they were in trouble.' Of the 'Jubilees' he said '. . .you do meet the black sheep among them, of course,

'Black Five' No 45473 rests in Perth shed on 27 June 1965, strikingly illuminated by the lowering evening sun. The quietness of the Sunday evening was only disturbed by the gentle hiss of steam and the occasional footplate noises elsewhere in the shed. *D. J. Hucknall*

and when you do . . . it is a devil of a job to get right – if you ever do succeed.'

Over the years some engines acquired good and bad reputations 'A1' No 60136 *Alcazar*, for instance, was a particularly rough-riding engine. No 60157 *Great Eastern* was fast, capable but ferocious at speed. Harold Gasson reported of the 'Castles' that No 5055 was the best in Old Oak Common, while No 5069 was the 'strongest'. Of the 'Kings', No 6014 was 'marvellous'. C. J. Allen records hearing 'A4' No 60011 described by a Perth driver as one of the finest engines he had been on in his life.

The practice, revived for a while in the immediate post-war years on certain parts of the railway system, of allocating an engine to one or two drivers led to care being lavished on certain engines so that they were in first-rate mechanical condition and performed accordingly. However, the introduction, initially on the LMS and later elsewhere, of the common-user locomotive led gradually to a deterioration in the appearance and condition of engines. There is a marvellous story in O. S. Nock's *Scottish Railways* (Nelson, 1961) concerning the 'A3' *Hyperion*. She was a real

black sheep, 'wouldn't steam, wouldn't run, rode badly . . . in fact a thorough dud. . .' She had been a common-user engine, but Norman McKillop was given her while his regular engine was in the Plant. Nock quotes McKillop's words: 'Both of us spent a miserable week together. . . The following week was ideal, a run to Perth with Glenfarg to climb . . . a place to tell engines and men where the troubles lay.'

With the competent handling and expert diagnostic skills of McKillop, one by one *Hyperion*'s problems were eliminated until she '. . . slipped out of Edinburgh like a ghost, didn't seem to touch the rails at all on the level and kicked the mountains beneath her with contemptuous ease. . .'

Over the years many magnificent portraits of locomotives have been taken by renowned photographers, but in my opinion the best are on shed, at the end of a run, with, to quote Harold Gasson, 'the gloss of her deep Brunswick green filmed with dust and flattened flies. A gentle trickle of water dribbled from the injector water pipe, splashing quietly on to the charred sleepers.'

Another 'Black Five' at Perth, No 45474, seen at close quarters. Clearly shown is the tablet-catching apparatus fitted to a good proportion of Scottish Class '5s'.

Carrying the power classification '5MT', the 'Black Fives' had a tractive effort of 25,455 lbs with an engine weight of 70½ tons. The first of the Class, No 5020, appeared from Crewe Works in 1934. The initial order was for 70 engines, but eventually 842 were built. No 45474 entered service in May 1943 and was withdrawn 23 years later. The 'Black Fives' were designed to be 'an engine that would go anywhere and do anything' (Rowledge and Reed in *The Stanier 4-6-0s*). '45671', a commentator whose articles on locomotive matters were both informative and highly readable, said of them (*Trains Illustrated*, January 1958), 'they were easy to fire and quite effective with a thick fire or a thin one, immune to fire-throwing unless grievously mishandled, steady on their feet – could a man want more?' *D. J. Hucknall*

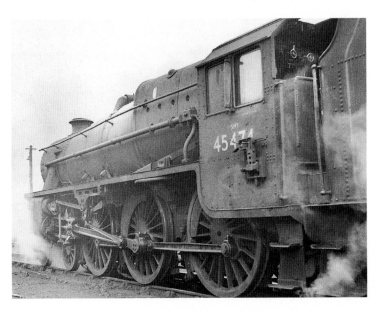

THE STEAM LOCOMOTIVE SHED

Cowlairs Works had a practice of painting the shed allocation of a locomotive on its buffer beam; examples of the labelling included 'Carlisle (Kingmoor)', 'Edgehill Liverpool', and 'Chester (Northgate)'. Some Perth 'Black Fives' were even identified with 'Perth (South)' perpetuating the name of the Caledonian Railway shed that had existed before the building of the LMS structure in the 1930s replaced it. In this photograph, taken inside Dumfries shed (67E) in March 1965, the shed-plate is at variance with the 'St Rollox' on the buffer beam. *D. J. Hucknall*

I had quite a soft spot for Dalry Road shed (64C); dating from 1911, it had been the principal shed of the Caledonian Railway in Edinburgh, and lay within a cramped triangular site between the lines from Princes Street station to Glasgow and to Perth. I first visited 64C on 23 January 1965. By then, its ex-Caledonian Railway engines had all gone and the predominant locomotives were 'Black Fives', 'B1s' and one or two 'J38s'. The shed was also used for servicing engines working West Coast trains out of Princes Street and then the occasional 'Coronation' Class would have been seen.

This close-up of the cab of 'Black Five' No 45162 on shed on 29 March 1965 shows clearly the grime and stains collected by an engine during its working days. Whilst at Ferryhill, No 45162 was the first recorded locomotive of its Class to work on the Deeside line, hauling a ballast train from Aberdeen to Peterculter and back on 23 November 1956. *D. J. Hucknall*

THE STEAM LOCOMOTIVE SHED

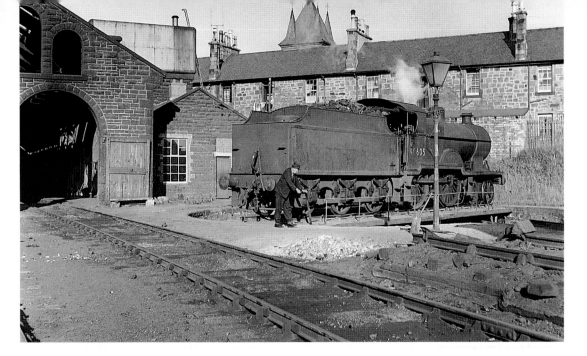

Above The evening of 16 July 1955 was swelteringly hot. Class '2P' 4-4-0 No 40605 (a Hurlford locomotive, sub-shedded at Muirkirk) has worked the 6.16 pm from Lanark, is being turned at Muirkirk shed and within 27 minutes will have to leave with the 7.15 pm train. Also on shed are three Caley 0-6-0s for mineral trains and an 0-4-4T. *W. A. C. Smith*

Below Seen with pin-point definition at Willesden shed on 11 June 1961 is 'Jubilee' No 45672 *Anson*. Her allocation (1A at this time) is painted on the smokebox door. *Anson* appeared to be a locomotive that was transferred with surprising

regularity. She was allocated to Bushbury in late February 1957, Camden in late November of the same year and went to Upperby shed, Carlisle, on 4 October 1958. She was transferred to Willesden at the beginning of March 1961.

In 1964 *Anson* had the dubious distinction of spending a great deal of unplanned time on the Southern Region. Arriving at Eastbourne shed on 19 June, she was used the following day on a local working to Haywards Heath. Later on the 20th she failed on the Newhaven-Glasgow car-sleeper. After being dumped on Brighton shed in the early hours of the 21st, she was eventually released on 2 July and returned slowly, light engine, to Willesden. *A. Swain*

Above An old friend encountered far from home – Ivatt Class '2' 2-6-0 No 46450 (a Grimesthorpe engine for many years and a Canklow engine in 1962) – photographed near Dumfries shed in March 1965. The Class '2s' were small engines (loco weight 47 tons 2 cwt) introduced in 1946 and equipped with rocker grates, hopper ashpans and, as indicated by 'SC', self-cleaning smokeboxes. I never realised how accepted and well-liked they were by enginemen. '45671' summed it up (*Trains Illustrated*, July 1958): '. . . an engine that could be driven hard, fired with a few bits of coal through which you could nearly see the grate, and that would steam well enough to suit the most fastidious'. *D. J. Hucknall*

Above right The 'B1s' were the LNER's equivalent of the LMS's 'Black Fives' – fast engines, capable of long and heavy work. Although slightly more powerful than the Class '5s' (tractive effort 26,878 lbs at 85 per cent boiler pressure), they were never praised to the same extent, possibly because there were only half the number. Nevertheless, in the 1948 locomotive exchanges 'B1' No 61251 *Oliver Bury* destroyed the myth of the superiority of the 'Black Five'.

Withdrawals of the Class began in 1961 with Leicester's No 61085 (61057 had been scrapped earlier, having been damaged beyond repair in 1950). Even by 1966 almost 100 examples remained. Here, seen in early March 1965, one of 64A's 'B1s', No 61099, stands outside Dundee (Tay Bridge) shed. She was eventually withdrawn from Thornton Junction in November 1966 and was scrapped at Faslane in the following month. *D. J. Hucknall*

Right Sunday 31 January 1965 was a cheerless day at Dalry Road shed. Snow lay on the ground, the temperature was just above freezing and there was little wind to blow away the mists. Outside the shed 'B1' Class No 61245 *Murray of Elibank* stood buffered-up to a Clayton diesel. Inside, an engine was being lighted up and smoke seeped through an upper window.

For many years a Haymarket engine, No 61245 was transferred to Dalry Road in September 1963. The following December she went to 64A, remaining there for ten months before returning to 64C. Withdrawn in July 1965, No 61245 was scrapped by the Motherwell Machinery & Scrap Company three months later. *D. J. Hucknall*

Right Lowering clouds on 17 April herald yet another miserable day in the spring of 1965. Outside St Margarets shed are 'A4' Class No 60006 *Sir Ralph Wedgwood* and a 'B1'. On shed at the time were 'A4' No 60027 *Merlin*, 'V2s' Nos 60813 and 60816 and various 'B1s' and BR Standard 2-6-0s. The original *Sir Ralph Wedgwood* (No 4466) had been destroyed during an air raid on York, and No 4466 *Herring Gull* was renamed. Sent to Scotland from the Eastern Region at the end of October 1963, she emerged from store at Dalry Road on 13 May 1964 and was then sent to Aberdeen. *D. J. Hucknall*

Below From June 1937 until its transfer to Ferryhill some 25 years later, 'A4' Class No 60009 *Union of South Africa* was a Haymarket engine. In the 1950s she was a consistent performer on the most demanding of East Coast expresses such as the 'Capitals Limited' and its successor the 'Elizabethan'. During the summer of 1954 No 60009 worked the latter in two long spells (it appeared almost daily between early August and mid-September). As schoolboys at the time, my friends and I would cycle to Doncaster and from the vantage point of St James's Bridge would regularly see No 60009, beautifully cleaned, easing through the station at a steady 50-60 mph. Occasionally, we would see steam from its whistle form a bow wave on either side of the chimney just before its long, haunting note could be heard.

In their later years several 'A4s' were transferred to 61B to work the 3-hour trains between Glasgow and Aberdeen. Perth men, who worked them between Perth and Glasgow, had a high regard for No 60009 and her sister No 60011. Of the latter, it was reported (by C. J. Allen, *Modern Railways*, December 1962) that one 63A driver looked on her as the finest engine he had ever been on in his life. When No 60009 emerged from the Works in December 1963, she was to be the last steam locomotive to be overhauled at Doncaster.

No longer in quite such pristine condition, but still a capable engine, *Union of South Africa* is shown in this photograph at Perth shed in the spring of 1965. Withdrawn in June 1966, she was sold to J. B. Cameron one month later for preservation. *D. J. Hucknall*

The 'V2s' were good-looking engines, and when they were fitted with outside steam pipes, they were very much in the tradition of the 'A3s'. The first example of the Class appeared in 1936 and an article in the *Engineer* of that year suggested that the 'V2' was the most powerful locomotive on 10 wheels in Britain at that time. (J. F. Clay, 'The V2s' in *Essays in Steam*). They were very well received in Scotland, and Dundee's No 60836 looks particularly competent and striking as it stands outside St Margaret's shed. In summarising the work of the Class, John Clay pointed out that they had been a national asset before and during the Second World War but were less successful in the post-war conditions. 'There was, perhaps,' he said, 'too much racehorse blood in the "V2s" to make them successful hacks'. *D. J. Hucknall*

Below An extremely dirty 'A3' Class 4-6-2 No 60100 *Spearmint* stands in the yard at St Margarets in early 1965 – I never saw *Spearmint* in any other state. Some 13 years earlier, in the late summer of 1952, I had cycled to Doncaster and had seen her on shed prior to entering the locomotive works. As would be expected, she was filthy, but under the grime the blue livery, applied at an earlier works visit, was just visible. *Spearmint* spent the greater portion of her life (May 1930-April 1937; March-July 1938; December 1940-January 1963) allocated to Haymarket shed in Edinburgh, and was assigned to driver Norman McKillop. In one of his books, Charles Meacher states that McKillop had his fireplace decorated with a nameplate from *Spearmint* but that Mrs McKillop persuaded him 'to get rid of it'. No 60100 entered Darlington Works for repair in May 1965 but was condemned on 19 June and cut up. *D. J. Hucknall*

Above right 'A3' Class No 60051 *Blink Bonny* first entered service with the LNER as an 'A10', but was rebuilt in November 1945. For a few years, in the mid-1950s, she worked from Copley Hill shed (May 1954-Sept 1957), dashing up and down the East Coast Main Line on that shed's turns (the up 'White Rose', 'Queen of Scots', the 7.50 am down from King's Cross, etc). From September 1957 until her condemnation in November 1964, she was sent to the North East, mainly allocated to either Gateshead or Darlington sheds. In this photograph, taken on 2 May 1964, No 60051 is seen outside York mpd. Because she was working a special she had been embellished with silver-painted hinge-straps on the smokebox door. *D. J. Hucknall*

Right No 60052 *Prince Palatine*, converted from Gresley's 'A1' Class in August 1941, stands outside St Margarets on 7 February 1965, having been transferred there in late August 1963 from Gateshead. Clearly visible are the vacuum ejector exhaust pipe along the side of the boiler and the reversing rod below the running plate. No 60052 was eventually withdrawn on 17 January 1966, and stood outside the shed at St Margarets for some time afterwards before being sold for scrap in the following June. *D. J. Hucknall*

THE STEAM LOCOMOTIVE SHED

The magnificent lines of a Gresley 'A3' are shown in this classic shot of No 60041 *Salmon Trout* at Canal shed, Carlisle, on 20 September 1955. She would have worked down to Carlisle over the severely curved and graded Waverley route, toiling up the bank from Hawick and grinding round the curves to Riccarton before descending Liddesdale and eventually reaching Carlisle.

Canal shed had its own 'A3s' – including *Sir Visto, Bayardo, Coronach* and

Flamingo – which worked the line until they were condemned in the 1961-62 period. *Salmon Trout* entered service in December 1934 and from then until its transfer to 64A in July 1960 it was a Haymarket loco. By the time I knew 64A, No 60041 had been modified with a double chimney, trough smoke deflectors and, absurdly, a diagonal yellow stripe through her number. Incredibly, in visit after visit, week after week, I never saw her outside the shed. *K. C. H. Fairey*

THE STEAM LOCOMOTIVE SHED

The very impressive profile of Peppercorn 'A1' Class No 60131 *Osprey* is obvious in this close-up taken at Carlisle's other principal shed at Kingmoor. It shows clearly details such as the superheater header cover, the anti-vacuum valve and thin, almost fragile-looking, fluted piston and connecting rods. The smoke deflectors, set well forward and cut away to allow access to the lubricators and outside steam pipe, complement the double chimney. From 9 September 1951 No 60131 was a Grantham engine, but was moved to Copley Hill on 15 February 1953 and later transferred to Ardsley before its final move to Neville Hill on 28 July 1963. *D. J. Hucknall*

Below I love to see locomotives at close quarters. In this photograph of a pair of work-stained 'J27s' at North Blyth in July 1967, every detail of the front ends can be seen. The left-hand engine is No 65834, built by Robert Stephenson & Co in June 1909; it has a saturated boiler and short smokebox. Her sister has a frame extension at the front of the smokebox. They were big, powerful engines. As a student in Newcastle I would hear them blasting their way up from Manors station towards Jesmond. In their early days they were used to haul coal from the local collieries to the shipping staiths. *D. J. Hucknall*

Above right At 3 pm on Saturday 23 January 1965, the lowering sun illuminates the side of 'J38' No 65920 at Dalry Road. The 'J38s' performed miscellaneous shunting duties in and around Edinburgh. Before the Clayton Type 1 diesels took over the duty, towards the end of January, a 'J38' regularly carried out morning shunting duties in the sidings that ran between Salamander Street and Leith Links. *D. J. Hucknall*

Right Spring sunshine can reveal fascinating details on a locomotive. Here Class 'J37' (Reid NBR Class 'S') 0-6-0 No 64592, introduced in January 1919 and withdrawn in July 1965, stands in the shed yard at Grangemouth on 4 April 1965. The wonderful April sun has picked out the handle of the large handbrake on the footplate, the still-intact maker's plate on the centre splasher and what may be a balance weight just forward of the cab steps. The typical NBR tender, with a sheet metal coal guard behind its rails, is filled with good-quality coal. It also has two substantial patches at its base. *D. J. Hucknall*

THE STEAM LOCOMOTIVE SHED

THE STEAM LOCOMOTIVE SHED

Left The rebuilt Bulleid 4-6-2s were, in my opinion, very handsome locomotives, and this shot of 'West Country' Class No 34098 *Templecombe* taken at Banbury mpd on 2 January 1966 hardly does the Class justice. It is noteworthy, however, because it was one of the few presentable locomotives on the shed that day. The three ex-GWR engines (Nos 6916 *Misterton Hall*, 6930 *Aldersey Hall* and 7912 *Little Linford Hall*) also there were dreadfully dilapidated with the matt grey-brown colour that resulted from prolonged and deliberate neglect. Only a few years earlier I had been delighted by the 'Halls' at Banbury, and the dereliction of the three shocked and annoyed me. Banbury shed was closed almost exactly nine months after this photograph was taken. *D. J. Hucknall*

Above Although renowned for their free-steaming and the consistency of the work they produced, Bulleid's 'Pacifics',

as originally designed, were highly controversial engines. Externally, the air-smoothed casing over the whole of the upper part of the locomotive was unusual, but other features, such as the oil bath that enclosed the valve gear, proved troublesome and costly from the point of view of maintenance and accessibility.

To overcome these problems, the whole of the 'Merchant Navy' Class and a number of the 'West Country/Battle of Britain' Class were rebuilt with, among many features, an orthodox cylindrical smokebox, outside valve gear and large smoke deflectors. The result was a very impressive-looking locomotive as is clearly shown in this photograph of 'West Country' Class No 34097 *Holsworthy*, taken at Eastleigh in the 1960s. No 34097 had been a Brighton engine, moving to Exmouth Junction in November 1960. She was one of the final batch of 30 locomotives to be rebuilt in early 1961. *H. G. Usmar*

PORTRAITS

Above Rebuilt 'West Country' Class 'Pacific' No 34022 *Exmoor* and BR Standard Class '4' 4-6-0 No 75077 stand at Eastleigh. One of the fascinations about Eastleigh was the procession of engines bound for the Works. Reference to journals such as the *Railway Observer* shows that in the period 7 September to 5 October 1963, 36 locomotives arrived for attention, including five 'WC/BB' 'Pacifics'. One year later, from 3 August to 12 September, the tally was 38 locomotives, including three 'light Pacifics' and two 'Merchant Navys'.

Normally, an engine had a general or intermediate repair every 2-2½ years, the general repair involving a complete strip-down, including boiler removal. An intermediate involved stripping down the engine with the boiler in position. *H. G. Usmar*

Below Unrebuilt 'West Country' Class 4-6-2 No 34006 *Bude* is shown in the yard at Salisbury shed. The photographer, George Harrison, was particularly enthusiastic about the original Bulleid 'Pacifics', and was responsible for the compilation of a 'testimonial', based on railwaymen's comments on the locomotives, which was later presented to Oliver Bulleid. One former Locomotive Inspector of some 20 years' standing spoke of his 'duty and pleasure' to test the engines with heavy loads. Of his experiences on Western routes, accompanied by Western Inspectors, he wrote, 'These gentlemen have been astounded at the power and boiler efficiency maintained over very severe gradients in Devon and Cornwall.' *George Harrison*

THE STEAM LOCOMOTIVE SHED

Right Also at Eastleigh, 'Lord Nelson' Class 4-6-0 No 30850 *Lord Nelson* stands outside the shed. Towards the end of their careers, all the 'Nelsons' were allocated to 71A. Designed by R. E. L. Maunsell, the first of the Class was introduced in 1926. They were erratic performers, however, until Oliver Bulleid redesigned the front ends and gave them new cylinders, Lemaitre multiple-jet blastpipes and a large diameter chimney. Their performance improved dramatically but they were displaced from primary main-line duties by Bulleid's 'Pacifics'. Jim Evans, who had fired on the 'Nelsons', said of them, '. . . the Lord Nelsons were the complete steam locomotive. . . At speed the footplate set so high and far behind the rear wheel would roll at amazing angles, a sensation that would make the blood pound with excitement.' *D. J. Hucknall Collection*

Below Okehampton shed, a sub-depot of Exmouth Junction, was a one-road building located at the Exeter end of Okehampton station on the ex-SR route from Plymouth to Exeter; the station was sited on a hillside above the town which clustered in the Okement valley. Here we see 'N' Class 2-6-0 No 31834 standing in the shed yard on the morning of 4 April 1964. It was quite an unpleasant day and shortly after the shot was taken a sleet storm swept down from the hills with an intensity that made further photography pointless. *D. J. Hucknall*

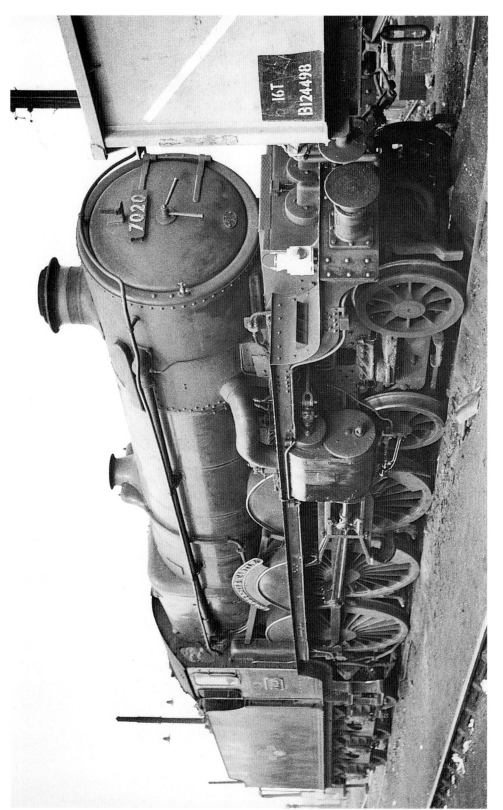

A portrait of 'Castle' Class No 7020 *Gloucester Castle* (81A) at Oxford shed; one of a group of post-war 'Castles' (Nos 5098/99, 7000-07 were completed by the Great Western Railway by July 1946). No 7020 was built by British Railways in the first half of 1949. It remained in its original condition until 1961 when it was fitted with a double chimney and blastpipe. It was transferred to 81A from Cardiff Canton at the beginning of 1957 and remained there until June 1964. It was withdrawn from Southall shed in September 1964. *D. J. Hucknall Collection*

THE STEAM LOCOMOTIVE SHED

Bristol Bath Road 'Castle' No 5069 *Isambard Kingdom Brunel* stands by the side of the coaling stage. This stage was 90 feet long and had three coal tips, while the tank above it held 135,000 gallons of water, pumped from the River Avon at Foxes Wood via a 15-inch diameter pipe.

This time the train reporting number is displayed in a metal frame carried on the smokebox door, as was the practice during the 1950s on certain passenger trains. I have not been able to identify the number 212 unambiguously; no such number is reported in the winter lists for 1956/7 or 1957/8, although from Whitehouse and Jenkinson (*From BR to Beeching*, Vol 1, Atlantic Transport Publishers 1990), train 212 appears to have been the summer 9.10 am Manchester (London Road) to Paignton. According to these authors the WR worked it from Bristol onwards and the sheds involved were usually 82A or Newton Abbot (83A). I have a photograph, however, showing a 'Castle' with '212' on the smokebox door at Reading (General) station. *H. G. Usmar*

THE STEAM LOCOMOTIVE SHED

Left Another wonderfully evocative picture of *Isambard Kingdom Brunel* at Bath Road. At this time she was a Laira engine; in 1952 she had been transferred to Bath Road from Old Oak Common in exchange for Bristol's solitary 'King', No 6000 *King George V*.

During the 1950s lightly loaded boat trains were run from Millbay Docks, Plymouth, to Paddington. On 7 October 1954 No 5069, with Driver Hammett and Fireman Luscombe in charge, set a then record time of 3 hrs 37 min to Paddington with a train of five coaches (171 tons tare). No 5069's performance was later equalled (20 October 1954) by No 5058 *Earl of Clancarty* with seven vehicles. *H. G. Usmar*

Above It is not difficult to understand the considerable pleasure that the locomotives of the former Great Western Railway have given to the railway enthusiasts of Britain, being associated in the minds of many with sunny childhood summers spent in Cornwall or Devon. This photograph of 'County' Class 4-6-0 No 1006 *County of Cornwall* was taken on 12 August 1957 at Penzance mpd when I was 16 years old. The afternoon sun shone on the copper band of the chimney and highlighted the 6 ft 3 in driving wheels, while the air had the 'summer' railway smell of creosoted sleepers and warm oil and metal mixed with salty sea breezes. *D. J. Hucknall*

Right Dalry Road on Saturday 20 March 1965, and on shed is St Rollox's BR Standard Class '5' No 73150. It was one of a series of 30 (Nos 73125-54) that were fitted with Caprotti valve gear at Derby Works and incorporated modifications that had been found necessary following experience with some of the 'Black Fives'.

The system appears to be highly complex. On top of the cylinder is the cambox containing the inlet/exhaust valve-actuating mechanism. The cambox drive comes from the intermediate coupled wheels using a worm gearbox. Another modification, compared to earlier Class '5s', was the rectangular-section coupling-rod.

The Standard Class '5s' could look impressive in lined-out black livery and this can be vaguely seen on the cabside. I can't recall, however, ever seeing an engine with such a filthy tender. *D. J. Hucknall*

Below Brand new, Standard Class '4MT' 2-6-4T No 80099 went to Plaistow to work on the London, Tilbury & Southend line. In November 1959 she was transferred to Tilbury, where she stayed until June 1962. Eventually reaching Machynlleth shed in July 1963, she spent the rest of her days working the beautiful lines of the former Cambrian Railways. Photographed at Aberystwyth shed, No 80099 still looks impressive. Although its lined-out livery is rather drab and dirty, against the foothills of Snowdonia or the wild saltings of the Dovey estuary it would still be a stirring sight. *D. J. Hucknall* Collection

THE STEAM LOCOMOTIVE SHED

6.
INTERLUDE:
TRAINSPOTTERS

I now realise that I was not much of a trainspotter. Looking once again through my old 'Combineds' (*Ian Allan ABC of British Railways Locomotives*, Combined Edition), I can see whole classes of locomotives where only a handful of the engines are marked off. I did, however, manage to see all the 'A1s' and 'A4s', but four 'A3s' (Nos 60074/87/99/111) evaded me – this in spite of living only 12 miles from Doncaster and spending hours sitting on wooden fences beside the East Coast Main Line at Bawtry and Ranskill. I fared little better with the 'Jubilees' – No 45552 and the Scottish engines rarely ran through Rotherham.

I suppose I lacked dedication. I was just not prepared to trek around the country, clambering over walls covered with broken glass, dashing for the cover of wagons and generally running the gauntlet of the railway authorities.

Steam sheds acted as magnets for trainspotters. According to the rules, visits to sheds had to be arranged officially and with some of the larger ex-LMS and ex-LNER depots, this was the only way. It would have been the very faint-hearted, however, who would not have used a convenient wall or attempted to sneak past the shed office to find a much sought-after engine. Sometimes the shed superintendent and his staff could be very understanding, and Sundays were excellent days for an unofficial look around.
'Castle' Class 4-6-0 No 5092 *Tresco Abbey* (82A, Bristol Bath Road) comes under scrutiny from a mature enthusiast. No 5092 was transferred to 82A in April 1958 from Reading shed (81D) as part of a re-shuffle in the allocations of 32 'Castles' among 13 depots which was aimed at dispersing high-mileage locos throughout the Western Region. Joining No 5092 at the time were No 5015 *Kingswear Castle*, No 5073 *Blenheim* and No 5090 *Neath Abbey*. D. J. Hucknall Collection

One drawback to lineside spotting was that it seemed to take an awfully long time to accumulate numbers, while sheds provided the opportunity to get them very quickly. Unfortunately, the same engines were always on the local sheds. Nevertheless, I would return time after time in the perpetual hope that a rare engine, particularly a 'namer', would be lurking among the usual tired-looking, uninspiring 'WDs', '8Fs' and '4Fs' of a freight-only depot like Canklow. Throughout my railway days I

never lost that feeling of anticipation as I approached a shed. It was for this reason that I used to enjoy Perth so much – and my expectations were usually fulfilled.

One solution to the dedicated locospotter's perennial problem of seeing every locomotive in Britain was to join one of the Locospotters Clubs that were so active in the 1950s and early '60s. Announcements of their activities would appear in magazines like *Trains Illustrated* – whirlwind tours of all the sheds in cities such as Birmingham, Manchester and Liverpool, or marathons covering swathes of the country. Peter Hands (see *Chasing Steam on Shed*, Barbryn Press Ltd 1982) chronicles his travels with the Railway Enthusiasts Club based in Birmingham, including a two-day trip to the North East of England in February (!) 1962 – '19 sheds visited,' he reported, '796 steam and 174 diesels seen, all for 55 shillings.'

The exploits of the serious trainspotter seem bewildering – dashes around Gateshead or Tebay sheds in the dead of night, for example. As Peter Hands recalls, '. . . we made an attempt to bunk Kingmoor in the dark but whilst in the shed yard we were warned by a driver that the police were present and so we gave up. . .'

In spite of my more tentative approach to the hobby, I had some marvellous times. Shed foremen at places such as Penzance and Banbury could be very understanding, and I shall always remember leisurely strolls around depots, taking the occasional photograph. My father used to be a keen bowls player, and once I travelled with the team to Wakefield for a match. The bowling green must have been very close to Wakefield mpd because I spent a long, sunny afternoon watching a seemingly endless parade of previously unseen locomotives (predominantly 'Austerities') trundle on and off the shed.

The afternoon drew to a perfect close, for just before I left I noticed the setting sun glinting on the burnished boiler of an approaching engine. As it drew nearer I could see that it was a 'Jubilee' (No 45717 from Bank Hall, in fact). It was a magnificent sight – an engine I had never seen before gliding past me, her piston rods gleaming in the last of the light.

Below York mpd on Saturday 2 May 1964 – with his gabardine raincoat (almost a uniform for the railway enthusiast of the period) sensibly belted, a trainspotter strolls past Worsdell 'J27' Class 0-6-0 No 65844, notebook in hand. For the railwayman striding purposefully in the opposite direction it was just another working day. *D. J. Hucknall*

Right A delighted boy gazes at the nameplate of 'Castle' Class 4-6-0 No 7018 *Drysllwyn Castle*. Railway sheds were wonderful because they presented an opportunity to see such outstanding locomotives at very close quarters indeed. It never seemed to be understood by the chroniclers that, as schoolboys, very few of us really had any appreciation of the mechanical aspects of railway engines, nor of the superb achievements of their crews. We would, however, travel miles to look at a 'rare' locomotive and underline it in our lists, and most of us can understand the feelings of this boy.

Previously an indifferent steamer, No 7018 had a double blastpipe and chimney fitted after which its performance was transformed. On one occasion, heading the up 'Bristolian' with Driver Russe (82A) in charge, No 7018 shifted a seven-coach train (260 tons gross) with, according to C. J. Allen (*Trains Illustrated*, September 1958), 'phenomenal' acceleration from Badminton to Wootton Bassett. He estimated that 102 mph 'at least' was reached at Little Somerford. *D. J. Hucknall Collection*

THE STEAM LOCOMOTIVE SHED

7.
REPAIRS

Repairs, often major ones, were part of the continuous struggle at a motive power depot to find enough engines to fulfil the allotted duties. Failures in service could cause great delay and inconvenience. In an awful period from mid-September 1953 to May 1954 King's Cross shed had, on average, one failure every 3½ days, with its 'A4s', 'A3s' and 'V2s'. Seventeen failures occurred with the 'Tees-Tyne Pullman' alone.

Some sheds were large enough and regarded as sufficiently important to have extensive facilities. Lathes, presses, wheel-drops, overhead cranes, forges, etc, were all available in these depots, and quite major repairs were carried out. At 'A' sheds such as Perth and Exmouth Junction, conditions were good – the repair shops were light and airy with appropriate equipment. Generally, however, there seemed to be no pattern – Oxford (81F) and Didcot (81E) had repair shops, while a main shed such as St Margarets had scant facilities. Alec Swain's photograph (opposite) of No 60004 at Haymarket with piston rings hanging from the buffers shows that even first-line depots had to cope with very basic conditions.

Maintenance work on locomotives could range from routine boiler washouts, valve and piston examinations to superheater repairs, hot axle-box correction and wheel-turning. Repairs could be carried out in the running shed, but usually this was needed for washouts. It was not uncommon at some sheds to see a locomotive in the yard jacked up on timbers, minus coupling-rods and surrounded by the usual fitter's paraphernalia – hammers, spanners, oxy-acetylene cylinders.

Richard Hardy (in *Steam in the Blood*, Ian Allan 1971) describes the primitive conditions that prevailed at some sheds. At Ipswich in the 1950s he recalls valve and piston examinations being carried out '. . . in the teeth of the easterly gales that blew straight in from the North Sea'. Describing Stewarts Lane main shed, he comments 'It was dark, ill-lit and low in the roof, and it was here that all the heavy repairs, washing out and servicing was carried out,' It must have been a great burden and perpetual headache to fitters and foremen to maintain skill and care under such conditions, for just one mistake could be costly, resulting in failure or accident.

At Crewe North the examination and repair shed, completed in 1959, was designed to provide all the facilities for specialist work on the ex-LMS 'Pacifics'. It was commandeered, however, as Crewe Diesel Depot, allegedly without seeing a single steam engine.

Above right Two of Haymarket's 'Pacifics', 'A4' Class No 60004 *William Whitelaw* and 'A1' Class No 60161 *North British* at Haymarket shed on Sunday 6 September 1959 – both are obviously out of action. No 60004 is undergoing an examination of its pistons and valves in the open; the piston and valve rings are hanging from the lamp brackets. Alec Swain, who took the photograph and who had been Chief Mechanical Foreman at Leicester shed, comments 'I would not have expected my fitters to work under those conditions.' *A. Swain*

Right Perth shed had some impressive repair facilities. Following the tradition of the Caledonian Railway, these were situated beside the engine shed, but with the stores, machine shop, etc between. Here one of 63A's own 'Black Fives', No 44799, is undergoing examination. The photograph was taken on 27 June 1965 and may record the end of the line for the engine; she was withdrawn in July. *D. J. Hucknall*

THE STEAM LOCOMOTIVE SHED

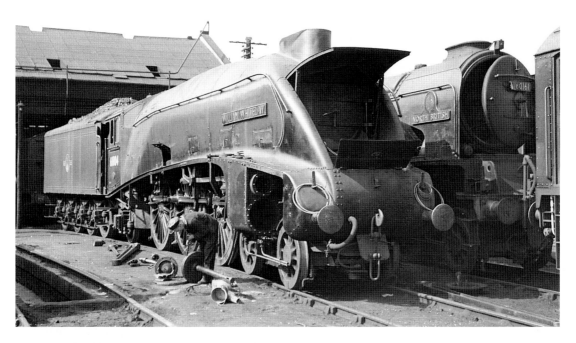

Engineering work in and around engine sheds was sometimes carried out with fairly makeshift equipment. It was not unusual to see cranes and pulleys attached to wooden posts lashed to running plates and buffer beams. In this photograph, taken at Ladyburn shed, Greenock, in September 1956, ex-Caledonian Railway 0-4-4T No 55267 and 4-4-0 No 54456 are providing power for a compressor and a small crane being used to repair the turntable. Ladyburn was an old shed, opened by the Caledonian Railway in 1884. In 1959 it had 39 engines, but by 1965 this had fallen to 12 and the shed eventually closed in December 1966. *W. A. C. Smith*

THE STEAM LOCOMOTIVE SHED

Right Ex-NBR Class 'J36' No 65234, being prepared for duty as a stationary boiler on the site of the old roundhouse at St Margarets on 7 February 1965; on the right is the usual style of stationary boiler mounted on a permanent base. Like the locomotive, the equipment used to carry out the work is a relic of railway practice at the beginning of the century. It consists of a spar carrying block and tackle and crudely lashed to the hand-rails, running-plate and spokes of the centre driving wheel. *D. J. Hucknall*

Below Slanting through a skylight, shafts of sun penetrate the gloom of St Margarets and illuminate 'V2' No 60846 undergoing repairs. Attached to her right-hand front lamp bracket is a 'Not to be moved' sign and the gas bottles by the buffers suggest that the fitters are not far away. At the beginning of 1965, when this photograph was taken, 64A had eight 'V2s'. They found regular work on Edinburgh to Perth passenger trains and were frequently used on goods trains on the Waverley route to Carlisle. *D. J. Hucknall*

Inside No 2 shed at Wellingborough on 29 April 1962 stands little ex-Midland Railway Johnson Class '2F' No 58148 from Coalville shed. She is receiving attention to her cylinders and valves prior to working a special railtour over the branch line from West Bridge, Leicester, to Desford Junction. At the time No 58148 was one of only three of the Class still running in normal service, all allocated to Coalville. They were retained to work the branch because they could pass through the narrow Glenfield tunnel. *K. C. H. Fairey*

THE STEAM LOCOMOTIVE SHED

Banbury shed – a brick-built four-road structure – was completed around late August 1908. During the Second World War an enormous increase in traffic resulted in Banbury becoming an extremely important and busy railway centre. Improvements to the shed were necessary and in 1943 a lifting shop was built, provided with a 68-foot pit and 50-ton engine hoist.

Taken almost exactly 50 years after the shed's opening, this photograph shows locomotives in the sidings between the shed and the lifting shop. Adjacent to the shed stands 'Castle' Class 4-6-0 No 7032 *Denbigh Castle* (81A). In the next siding are '94XX' Class 0-6-0PT No 8452, '57XX' Class 0-6-0PT No 3646 and '5600' Class 0-6-2T No 6627. Both the pannier tanks have been coaled, but the excess on the roofs has not been removed. This was not particularly good shed practice. *D. J. Hucknall*

REPAIRS

THE STEAM LOCOMOTIVE SHED

Left Old Oak Common 'Castle' No 7020 *Gloucester Castle* stands in a siding facing the repair shop at Oxford shed (81F). The raised roof section was to accommodate the shear legs which were used to lift a locomotive to remove the wheels. The usual paraphernalia associated with railway sheds in the days of steam – a discarded shovel, an abandoned wheelbarrow – can clearly be seen.

In the late 1950s Oxford shed had an allocation of 64 locomotives, including four 'Castles' of its own (Nos 5012/25/33 and 7008) that worked to Chester and Paddington. Oxford was a fascinating shed because main-line engines from the four regions of British Railways could regularly be seen there. It eventually closed in 1967, having served the needs of the railway system for well over one hundred years. *D. J Hucknall Collection*

Above With their fires completely dropped, 'Grange' No 6800 *Arlington Grange* and a couple of 'Halls' stand on one of the four roads inside Penzance shed. While an engine was cold, repairs that could not otherwise be considered were carried out. From the pools of water and the abandoned hose, it seems that one engine at least has had a boiler washout. The smell of a locomotive shed is hard to describe. Walking between the engines, waves of smells are encountered – here paraffin, there lubricating oil, next saturated steam – all contributing to the indescribable atmosphere. *D. J. Hucknall*

8.
READY TO GO

Over the years, such respected authors as O. S. Nock and C. J. Allen travelled the length and breadth of the country timing trains, and many engine crews acquired well-deserved reputations for distinguished work on Britain's top expresses as a result of their articles and books. The East Coast Main Line had, for example, drivers such as Hoole and Hailstone at King's Cross and Swan and Nairn at Haymarket. The Southern Region had Tutt and Gingell at Stewarts Lane.

Although receiving much less publicity, drivers such as Carruthers and Stalker (Carlisle Upperby), Newcombe and Hammett (Laira) and Edwards (Kentish Town), and many, many others, were responsible for outstanding runs on their allotted routes. It is the way of the world, however, that their partners, the firemen – often shifting tons of coal on a long, fast run – received much less attention.

While a locomotive was running the duties of the crew were fairly clear cut. It was the driver's responsibility to run his train safely, economically and to schedule, while the fireman was concerned with the efficient generation of steam. Both before and after the journey, however, the engine was in the hands of firedroppers, cleaners, boilersmiths and other essential members of the shed staff.

Steam locomotive depots employed considerable numbers of people. According to H. G. Forsythe (*Men of Steam*, Atlantic Books 1982), King's Cross shed employed 1,100. Of the 1,000 at Old Oak Common, approximately 800 were drivers and firemen. Career progression in the old days of steam was extremely slow. In the inter-war period it could have taken 30 years to work through the ranks from cleaner to driver and onwards. It was supposed to introduce a man to his profession.

At the beginning of his work the driver of an engine would collect from the shed stores cylinder oil and lubricating oil. The fireman would obtain a shovel, coal hammer and various tools, lamps and other necessary equipment. Generally the engine was partially prepared before the crew arrived. The fire would be relatively small, and the first task of the fireman was to built it up by spreading it over the grate and adding fairly large lumps of coal. It was not unusual to add almost a ton before departure from the shed. The smoke produced by a recently lit fire did not have the pleasant smell of that from a hot locomotive. It had a choking, sooty quality and, because the blower could not be used, it evolved slowly from the chimney to be wafted by any vague wind.

While the fire was burning through, the fireman would tighten the smokebox door, check the cleanliness of the ashpan and satisfy himself that injectors, gauges and the blower were working. The driver would be examining the locomotive in great detail, topping up mechanical lubricators and oiling vital components.

D. J. Fleming, who had been closely associated with St Philips Marsh shed, remembers early Monday mornings '. . . when you could not see across the shed with all the numerous engines being prepared for their duties. . . I remembered the atmosphere of it all; flare lamps glowing in the dark; flickering shadows; the sound of blowers operating, the singing of safety valves . . . the thud of coal picks, the ringing of shovels. . .'

THE STEAM LOCOMOTIVE SHED

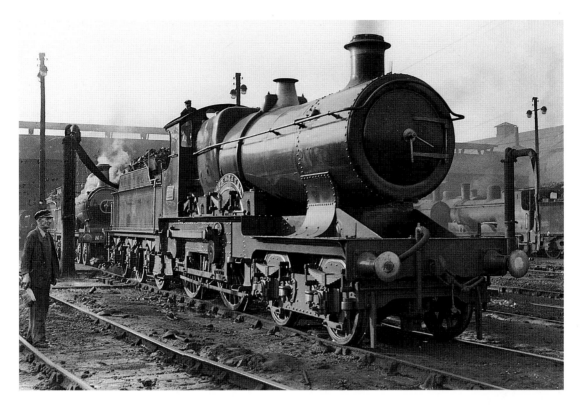

Above In connection with the Scottish Industries Exhibition that was held at Kelvin Hall, Glasgow, a programme of special excursions was organised during the first fortnight in September 1959. Four preserved pre-1923 locomotives (*City of Truro, Gordon Highlander*, No 123, and *Glen Douglas*) were involved. On 5 September *City of Truro* and *Gordon Highlander* had hauled one of the specials from Aberdeen to Glasgow, and are shown here being prepared for the 7.30 pm return at Polmadie shed under the gaze of a crew member. *W. A. C. Smith*

Right When new, Peppercorn 4-6-2 No 60530 *Sayajirao* was stationed at King's Cross mpd, moving to New England shed in December 1948. On 9 January 1950 she went to Haymarket shed in Edinburgh, staying there for over ten years. Late in her career, the transfers were frequent – St Margarets (16 October 1961), Polmadie (15 September 1963), Dundee (31 July 1964). In this photograph No 60530 is shown being serviced at St Margarets. In the background a DMU rushes past on the main line. *D. J. Hucknall*

Waiting at Polmadie shed on 24 June 1960 to work overnight Anglo-Scottish trains are Bank Hall's 'Jubilee' No 45717 *Dauntless*, Camden's 'Coronation' No 46246 *City of Manchester* and Polmadie's 'Coronation' No 46224 *Princess Alexandra*. In the 1950s there were five sleeping-car departures from Glasgow Central between 9.25 and 11.30 pm – three to London, one to Birmingham and a combined Liverpool/Manchester. The Stanier 'Pacifics' were responsible for most of the London and Birmingham workings while 'Royal Scots', 'Jubilees' and 'Clans' (later 66A 'Britannias') were in charge of the Lancashire trains. The 66A '8P' on the Glasgow-Birmingham trains was changed either at Carlisle or Crewe. *W. A. C. Smith*

THE STEAM LOCOMOTIVE SHED

Right The essence of the engine shed has been captured, as it has in most of his photographs in this book, by Bill Smith. Taken on 15 April 1963 it shows 'Clan' 4-6-2 No 72006 *Clan McKenzie*, Ivatt 2-6-0 No 46467 and Stanier 'Black Five' No 44795 outside Stranraer shed. From the beginning of the Second World War until 1952 the Glasgow-Stranraer line was worked by 'Jubilees' and 'Black Fives'.

In 1952, however, the BR 'Clans' began work on an intensive turn from Carlisle involving the 3.16 am Carlisle-Stranraer Harbour parcels, the 11.44 am Stranraer-Glasgow, 5.10 pm Glasgow-Stranraer and the 12.10 am Stranraer Harbour-Carlisle parcels. The poor old 'Clans' were indifferent performers. According to Derek Cross, writing in *The Railway Magazine* in July 1952, with trains heavier than three to five vehicles they steamed badly and slipped significantly, particularly on the climb from Creetown to Gatehouse of Fleet. *W. A. C. Smith*

Below Beattock bank is the name given to the 12-mile-long climb, mostly at 1 in 75, through the 'silent miles of wind-bent grasses' between the Lowther Hills and the heights of Tweedsmuir on the Carlisle-Glasgow main line. Such was the severity of the climb on the south side that, in the days of the steam locomotive, many northbound trains would have to opt for banking assistance at Beattock station prior to the gruelling climb ahead.

Over the years ex-Caledonian Railway 4-6-2Ts and 0-4-4Ts were used as bankers, but, towards the end, Fairburn Class '4MTs' were the preferred type. Here, on 4 August 1962, bankers Nos 42214 and 42239 stand outside the shed. On my only visit to Beattock in March 1965, Nos 42060, 42214, 42688 and 42693 were 'on shed'. The shed survived until the end of steam on the Scottish Region, but in May 1967 it closed and its last two locomotives went for scrap. *W. A. C. Smith*

Britannia' 'Pacific' No 70053 *Moray Firth* was completed (together with No 70052) at Crewe Works around late August 1954, and the pair were sent to Polmadie to join Nos 70050/51. Initially they joined the 'Clans' on workings between Glasgow and Liverpool such as the 7.24 pm arrival at Liverpool (Exchange) from Glasgow and the 9.43 am return. Within a couple of months, however, they had virtually ousted the 'Clans'.

In October 1958 No 70053 was transferred to Holbeck where it was used to work trains such as the 'Thames-Clyde Express'. It was transferred to the Midland Region in August 1962, and by October 1965 the former Polmadie 'Britannias' were found working from Banbury together with a motley collection of locomotives including '8Fs' and 'Black Fives'.

When this photograph was taken on 2 January 1966, Banbury had a further nine months before closure, whereafter *Moray Firth* and her sisters returned to the north once more, this time to Kingmoor. *D. J. Hucknall*

On the afternoon of 6 August 1958 '9F' Class 2-10-0 No 92226 slowly draws away from Banbury shed, cylinder cocks open and fierce jets of steam piercing the air. The '9Fs' were allocated to Banbury to replace some Stanier '8F' 2-8-0s that had been transferred there in 1955.

Ironstone, originating either in Northamptonshire or in the wolds on the Leicestershire/Nottinghamshire borders, was an important commodity required by the steel industry of South Wales. Motive power for the ironstone trains between Banbury and South Wales was provided by the '9Fs' that worked to Cardiff, Llanwern and Severn Tunnel Junction. Banbury's '9Fs' were not used exclusively on these trains and were also to be found on trains to Birkenhead and Reading. *D. J. Hucknall*

Standard Class '5' 4-6-0 No 73106 (63A) looks quite magnificent as she stands at Eastfield shed, Glasgow, on 9 June 1960. Fresh from Cowlairs Works, she would have been running in and the crew appear to be concerned with the right-hand injector exhaust. Also in the picture, on the right, one of Hurlford's Standard Class '3' 2-6-0s, No 77019, appears to have recently emerged from the Works. *W. A. C. Smith*

THE STEAM LOCOMOTIVE SHED

9.
DUTIES

The function of the shed and its personnel was to provide men and locomotives to carry out the allotted tasks. Enginemen at a shed were divided into 'links', and the duties covered by each link were well defined. A medium-sized shed such as Banbury would have links to deal with the vacuum-piped goods trains, excursions, crew relief for goods trains passing through the area, branch-line trains, etc. A large shed such as St Margarets would have to deal with fast freights on the East Coast Main Line or the Waverley route, dock shunting, routine work in colliery sidings, empty stock, and so on. Depending on the shed, its duties, its allocated engines and even the weather, footplate work could be exhilarating and fulfilling, or grim and arduous, delightfully easy or stultifyingly boring.

Record-breaking performances on express trains have been chronicled extensively over the years by authors such as P. Ransome Wallis and O. S. Nock, but often the most telling accounts of locomotive work come from the enginemen themselves. Harold Gasson (in *Nostalgic Days*, OPC 1980) describes so well the satisfaction of a job well done. After a long hard struggle with a poor engine and a heavy freight, the end of the duty was in sight. He recalls:

'As the sinking sun caught us, that old locomotive became a thing of beauty . . . the shadows of the engine ran with us in soft outline, sliding over the meadows and cornfields, slipping over hedges and ditches . . . the feather of steam from the safety valve, a wisp of steam escaping from the whistle. . .'

A highly readable account of a footplate trip from Water Orton, Birmingham, to Carlisle with a freight train hauled by '9F' No 92165 is given by P. Ransome Wallis (*Trains Illustrated*, November 1959).

Dusty, dirty Class '2F' 0-6-0 No 57326 acts as pilot on Motherwell shed on 2 March 1963. In a large depot such as this, the loco shunt was a very necessary duty, involving replacing filled wagons on the ashpit with empties and assembling wagons for the coaling plant.

The '2F' 'Jumbos' were introduced in 1883 as the standard goods design of Dugald Drummond. In total 244 locomotives were produced (by Drummond and his successors) in the period to 1897. As late as 1959, nearly half the stock was still in existence.

The winter of 1962/63 was awful and several other Caley veterans were in steam on that day in March. They had been returned to service because of the

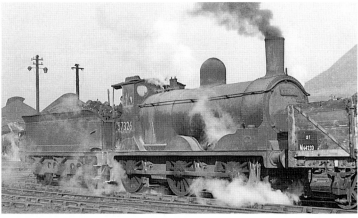

unreliability of the Clayton diesels in the freezing weather. *W. A. C. Smith*

'From Settle Junction,' he recounts, 'this was one of the most memorable trips ever made on an engine in Britain. With the regulator fully open and the cut-off brought back by stages from 15 to 40 per cent, No 92165 roared up the long bank . . . throwing smoke and coal dust in clouds from the chimney but with a perfect beat. . . A crisp, clear, moonlit night added beauty and exhilaration to our progress, and the shadow of the engine was often clearly defined on the moorland hills.'

Rapid progress is necessary for Robinson Class 'O4/1' 2-8-0 No 63736 (built August 1912; withdrawn August 1963) as she is occupying the up East Coast Main Line near Ranskill on the evening of 14 June 1957. The fact that the first four vans of this freight train were from the SNCF was unusual. Tender-first running was uncomfortable for the crew because of coal dust blowing from the tender. *D. J. Hucknall*

THE STEAM LOCOMOTIVE SHED

'And what a joy it has been to travel behind a "Duchess" storming up Shap on a moonlit night . . . that crisp, deep and beautifully even exhaust echoing across the fells.' This sentence, taken from an article by D. F. Tee in the *Railway Observer* of November 1964 expresses perfectly the feelings of many towards these superb locomotives. Workings such as the 'Mid-day Scot' demanded carefully prepared engines in first-rate condition. In this photograph of 'Coronation' Class No 46249 *City of Sheffield* at Glasgow Central on 22 April 1954, this aspect of shed work is brilliantly exemplified. The tender, coaled with fuel of exceptional uniformity and trimmed to perfection, and the locomotive, with the safety valves lightly lifting, speak volumes for the care and competence of the shed staff at Polmadie. *W. A. C. Smith*

THE STEAM LOCOMOTIVE SHED

Left Looking for the 'right away' from King's Cross station, a crew member leans well out of the cab of 'A1' No 60156 *Great Central*. This Class was one of the most consistent and reliable ever to run on Britain's railways. No 60156 was one of six 'A1s' allocated to Grantham shed's top link in the mid-1950s when that depot was responsible for many East Coast Main Line expresses, including the down 'Flying Scotsman', 'Aberdonian', and up 'Heart of Midlothian'. In September 1956, when through workings between Newcastle and King's Cross were reintroduced, Grantham's 'A1s' were sent to King's Cross shed. In the few years it spent there, No 60156 was possibly the shed's most dependable locomotive. One of her regular drivers was Horace Duckmanton whose outstanding work over the years was admirably highlighted by P. J. Coster (see *SLS Journal*, August/September 1968) and complemented by this remarkable locomotive. *D. J. Hucknall Collection*

Above Britain's railwaymen worked their way slowly through the hierarchy from engine cleaning to firing to driving. It was a process that took many years and involved arduous and sometimes dangerous work at unsociable hours. They were men who were respected in their communities and who contributed immeasurably to the wealth of the country. In this undated photograph, the photographer has captured superbly two unknown railwaymen. Doubtless, and justifiably, proud of their gleaming 'Hall', No 7908 *Henshall Hall* (Tyseley), they await the 'right away' from Reading. *H. G. Usmar*

Below With a background of Bristol Bath Road shed, final preparations are made to 'Castle' Class 4-6-0 No 5003 *Lulworth Castle* prior to departure from Temple Meads station. A complement of trainspotters has converged on the engine and one of them is about to 'footplate' the 'Castle'.

The fireman is attending to his fire with a dart. Part of the art of the fireman was to deal with the clinker that blocked the airspaces in the grate and prevented air admitted through the dampers from reaching the fire. With the dart he would break up and dislodge any clinker, and a pricker would be used to clear out airspaces in the grate. The best safeguard was to spread a bucketful of firebrick or limestone over the grate before the fire was built up. *H. G. Usmar*

THE STEAM LOCOMOTIVE SHED

10.
THE END

In the face of increasing dieselisation and electrification, the decline of steam and, with it, that of the steam motive power depot was inexorable. Examples from a list of sheds closed to steam at the time made depressing reading: Cricklewood (14.12.64); Reading (4.1.65); Bushbury (12.4.65); Crewe North (14.6.65); Dalry Road (3.10.65); Banbury (3.10.66); Tyseley (7.11.66), and so on.

Some closures had significance far beyond the importance of the shed. For example, when Nuneaton's depot closed in June 1966 there

On the morning of 2 March 1965 the former Gateshead 'A4' No 60016 *Silver King* stands in store at the rear of Perth shed. Having been transferred to St Margarets on 28 October 1963, within two weeks she was moved to Ferryhill. Condemned some 17 days after this photograph was taken, she was scrapped in May 1965.

Perth mpd was a typical 1930s LMS structure, made of brick, steel and corrugated sheet. It had replaced two Perth sheds (North and South) that had been used to house Highland Railway and Caledonian Railway engines respectively. *D. J. Hucknall*

were no steam depots south of Crewe on the London Midland main line via the Trent Valley. When Tyseley was closed in November 1966, steam on the Western Region's West Midlands lines was largely confined to the Wolverhampton area (Oxley shed continued with steam operations). In sharp contrast, the scrapyards became increasingly crowded (at Barry Docks at the end of July 1966 there were 172 locomotives including six 'Merchant Navies' and eight 'Manors').

I left Scotland in late 1965, and by the end of 1966 the elimination of steam was very advanced. Few trains were steam-hauled and even then they were restricted to perhaps three operations, including coal traffic from Fife and various freight/parcels workings to and from Carlisle. My shed visits became fewer and fewer

as the condition of locomotives deteriorated, and I feel that my last sight of a British Railways steam locomotive in revenue-earning service was of an 'Austerity' (almost inevitably) pulling empty mineral wagons through Gateshead.

Today almost all the railway sheds that were once so important to the economic life of Britain have gone forever. True, there are here and there examples of intact working sheds (usually, as in the cases of Didcot and Carnforth, associated with preservation societies), but it is easy to assume that bulldozers and tarmac have removed forever any trace of their existence. If, however, we are prepared to look carefully, in the weeds and shrubs, near some old track, the outline of the shed building or the coaling stage or the turntable pit may yet be found.

The evening sun on 3 June 1963 dapples the boiler of 'A1' Class 4-6-2 No 60154 *Bon Accord*, also in store at York South shed. *Bon Accord* was one of five 'A1s' (Nos 60153-7) fitted with roller bearings. During their working lives, the five were wonderfully reliable, Nos 60154 and 60155 *Borderer* being outstanding. On her withdrawal No 60154 had covered 1,035,000 miles. On the right stands stored 'V2' No 60831. Transferred to 50A in September 1959 from the former Great Central depot at Woodford Halse, she survived until December 1966, to be scrapped in the following February by Drapers in Hull. *D. J. Hucknall*

THE STEAM LOCOMOTIVE SHED

Above Without prospect of work, covered with grime and denied even their nameplates, a line of four 'Jubilees' stands at Carlisle Kingmoor in March 1965; shown here are Nos 45629 *Straits Settlements*, 45742 *Connaught* and 45574 *India*.

Connaught, a Bushbury engine for many years, was fitted with a double chimney from mid-1940 until November 1955 and was a very economical, freely steaming engine, figuring prominently on the 2-hour Wolverhampton/Birmingham-Euston trains. At the start of the 1959 winter timetables, all Bushbury's 'Jubilees', including No 45742, were transferred to Carlisle Upperby. *India*, among other things, was notable for having hauled the last LMS train to arrive at Euston on 31 December 1947; she drew in at 11.55 pm, and at midnight British Railways came into existence. *Connaught* was withdrawn in May 1965; *India* survived for another year. *D. J. Hucknall*

Right After its very last run in August 1967, 'Battle of Britain' Class No 34060 (formerly *25 Squadron*) has been left outside Salisbury shed. The locomotive is in dreadful external condition and a lack of manpower is further reflected in the track-side piles of ash and clinker. Already the ubiquitous rose-bay willow-herb is appearing amongst the debris. Salisbury shed was eventually used as a collection point for many former Southern Region locomotives awaiting scrapping. *George Harrison*

THE END

THE STEAM LOCOMOTIVE SHED

Left The end at Okehampton – gone are the steam locomotives, gone is the shed. The only things remaining by July 1965 are the water column and, of course, a wagon of ash. *D. J. Hucknall*

Above Its services long dispensed with and now marked by passing birds, '45XX' Class 2-6-2T No 5537 stands in Penzance shed yard at Long Rock in August 1963. For a long time she had been stationed at Truro, working the branch line to Falmouth with her sisters. It was the increasing use of diesel multiple units in Devon and Cornwall during the summer of 1961 that accelerated the withdrawal of the 'Prairie' tanks. No 5537 moved to Penzance in January 1962 and was withdrawn from that shed in the following August.

Looking at her, one remembers a verse from 'Dilton Marsh Halt' by John Betjeman:

'And when all the horrible roads are finally done for,
And there's no more petrol left in the world to burn,
Here to the Halt from Salisbury and from Bristol
Steam trains will return.'

D. J. Hucknall

THE END

APPENDIX
SELECTED SHED VISIT LOGS

I have a passion for shed visit logs. As I pore over them, I can almost see an 'A1' at St Margarets, two or three 'Coronations' at Perth; perhaps a grey, foggy day, perhaps a spring day with clouds being driven across the sky and flashes of sun transforming the rows of locomotives.

My own records are few and far between – one or two from Penzance and Banbury in the late 1950s, lists of Scottish shed visits in the 1964/5 period – not for me the carefully collected numbers in a hard-bound notebook, more the hastily torn scrap of paper as I leapt from my bicycle and rushed along a line of locomotives.

Obviously only a few of the following logs are my own. For the most part they have been compiled by Steve Turnbull of the Engine Shed Society; he compiles such records as a labour of love and they provide invaluable 'snapshots' of what was once an essential part of the life of this country. In choosing the logs I have tried to find ones that are as near as possible contemporary with the photographs in this book. In some cases, however, they are included because I liked the shed and I should have loved to have been there taking the numbers.

Aberdeen (Ferryhill)

16 November 1963

'Black 5' 4-6-0:	44705, 44720, 45136, 45359, 45400
'A4' 4-6-2:	60011 *Empire of India*, 60012 *Commonwealth of Australia*
'V2' 2-6-2:	60898, 60970, 60973
'B1' 4-6-0:	61244 *Strang Steel*, 61347, 61400
Standard '4' 2-6-0:	76104, 76107
Standard '2' 2-6-0:	78045
'Austerity' 2-8-0:	90041, 90117, 90444, 90640, 90705

30 July 1965

'Black 5' 4-6-0:	44704, 44705, 44794, 44879
'A4' 4-6-2:	60009 *Union of South Africa*, 60024 *Kingfisher*, 60026 *Miles Beevor*, 60027 *Merlin*
'A3' 4-6-2:	60052 *Prince Palatine*
'B1' 4-6-0:	61404
Standard '5' 4-6-0:	73056, 73152
'Austerity' 2-8-0:	90596
Diesels:	D357, D359, D1851, D3546, D5125, D5306, D5314, D5324

Bristol (Bath Road)

10 August 1958

'County' 4-6-0:	1003 *County of Wilts*, 1009 *County of Carmarthen*, 1011 *County of Chester*
'1400' 0-4-2T:	1454
'5700' 0-6-0PT:	3632, 3748, 3759, 7733, 8741, 8747
'Castle' 4-6-0:	4075 *Cardiff Castle*, 4079 *Pendennis Castle*, 4086 *Builth Castle*, 5048 *Earl of Devon*, 5055 *Earl of Eldon*, 5068 *Beverston Castle*, 7007 *Great Western*, 7011 *Banbury Castle*, 7015 *Carn Brea Castle*, 7018 *Drysllwyn Castle*, 7030 *Cranbrook Castle*, 7034 *Ince Castle*, 7035 *Ogmore Castle*
'5100' 2-6-2T:	4131 (for repair), 5186, 5188
'4500' 2-6-2T:	4595, 5511, 5527, 5529, 5546, 5553, 5565, 5566, 9623, 9626, 9769
'Hall' 4-6-0:	4927 *Farnborough Hall*, 4932 *Hatherton Hall*, 4960 *Pyle Hall*, 4975 *Umberslade Hall*, 4996 *Eden Hall* (repair), 5919 *Worsley Hall*,

5945 *Leckhampton Hall*, 5964 *Wolseley Hall*, 5977 *Beckford Hall*, 5987 *Brocket Hall*, 6957 *Norcliffe Hall*

'6100' 2-6-2T:	6107, 6137
'4300' 2-6-0:	6323, 6353
'Grange' 4-6-0:	6809 *Burghclere Grange*, 6874 *Haughton Grange*
'Modified Hall' 4-6-0:	6993 *Arthog Hall*
'9400' 0-6-0PT:	9488
Class '2' 2-6-2T:	41202
Standard '3' 2-6-2T:	82040, 82041, 82042, 82043

Bristol (St Philips Marsh)

27 July 1962

'County' 4-6-0:	1005 *County of Devon*, 1011 *County of Chester*, 1024 *County of Pembroke*
'1361' 0-6-0ST:	1365
'2251' 0-6-0:	2291, 3218
'2800' 2-8-0:	2822, 3830, 3837, 3854
'5700' 0-6-0PT:	3623, 3677, 3766, 4619, 4660, 7729, 8746, 8790, 8795, 9601
'Castle' 4-6-0:	4077 *Chepstow Castle*, 5040 *Stokesay Castle*, 5089 *Westminster Abbey*, 7018 *Drysllwyn Castle*
4200 2-8-0 T:	4258, 5213
'Hall' 4-6-0:	4914 *Granmore Hall*, 4918 *Dartington Hall*, 4922 *Enville Hall*, 4933 *Himley Hall*, 4942 *Maindy Hall*, 4947 *Nanhoran Hall*, 4956 *Plowden Hall*, 4968 *Shotton Hall*, 4999 *Gopsal Hall*, 5908 *Moreton Hall*, 5914 *Ripon Hall*, 5918 *Walton Hall*, 5926 *Grotrian Hall*, 5975 *Winslow Hall*, 6914 *Langton Hall*, 6919 *Tylney Hall*
'5600' 0-6-2T:	5640, 6654

'4300' 0-6-0:	6319, 6358, 6362, 6364, 7338
'6400' 0-6-0PT:	6408
'Grange' 4-6-0:	6809 *Burghclere Grange*, 6811 *Cranbourne Grange*, 6814 *Enborne Grange*, 6869 *Resolven Grange*
'Modified Hall' 4-6-0:	6982 *Melmerby Hall*, 7901 *Dodington Hall*, 7907 *Hart Hall*, 7924 *Thornycroft Hall*
Class '2' 2-6-2T:	41208, 41209
Class '2' 2-6-0:	46517
Standard '3' 2-6-2T:	82035, 82037, 82038
'9F' 2-10-0:	92248
Diesel:	D3503

Canklow

Sunday 1 July 1962

'4MT' 2-6-0:	43037
'4F' 0-6-0:	44089
'5MT' 4-6-0:	44846, 45434
'Patriot' 4-6-0:	45536 *Private W. Wood VC*
'Jubilee' 4-6-0:	45615 *Malay States*, 45658 *Keyes*
'8F' 2-8-0:	48008, 48150, 48141, 48178, 48216, 48265, 48283, 48346, 48351, 48397, 48508, 48652, 48772
'B1' 4-6-0:	61083, 61093, 61165, 61316
Standard '5' 4-6-0:	73016, 73046, 73068, 73074, 73130
Standard '4' 2-6-0:	76088
'Austerity' 2-8-0:	90276, 90391, 90414, 90471, 90719

Carlisle (Canal)

15 August 1954

Class '4' 2-6-0:	43139

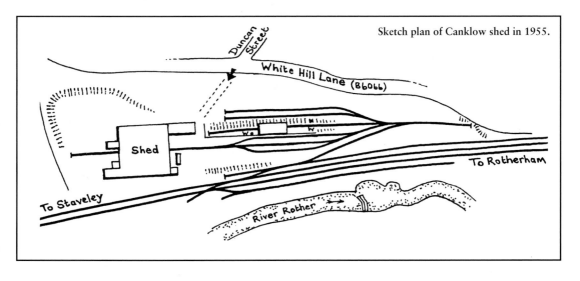

Sketch plan of Canklow shed in 1955.

'A3' 4-6-2:	60037 Hyperion, 60068 Sir Visto, 60093 Coronach
'V2' 2-6-2:	60840, 60919, 60933
'B1' 4-6-0:	61199, 61217, 61219, 61239, 61395
'K3' 2-6-0:	61854, 61855, 61858, 61882, 61898, 61936, 61937
'D49' 4-4-0:	62732 Dumfries-shire
'J35' 0-6-0:	64471, 64499, 64511, 64526
'J39' 0-6-0:	64733, 64877, 64880, 64884, 64888, 64898, 64912, 64930, 64932, 64948, 64964
'J36' 0-6-0:	65216 Byng, 65293, 65304, 65312, 65321
'C15' 0-6-0T:	67458, 67474, 67481
'N15' 0-6-2T:	69155, 69174, 69215
'Austerity' 2-8-0:	90539
Diesels:	12084, 12086

Carlisle (Kingmoor)

20 April 1962

Class '4' 2-6-4T:	42233, 42304
'Crab' 2-6-0:	42757, 42801, 42882, 42884, 42901, 42906, 42907
Class '4' 2-6-0:	43027, 43103
'3F' 0-6-0:	43622
'4F' 0-6-0:	43902, 44008, 44009, 44181, 44183, 44277, 44451
'Black 5' 4-6-0:	44666, 44668, 44669, 44673, 44675, 44725, 44878, 44883, 44898, 44899, 44953, 44958, 44969, 44974, 44993, 45072, 45138, 45168, 45334, 45363, 45365, 45457, 45460, 45466, 45481, 45484
'Jubilee' 4-6-0:	45566 Queensland, 45640 Frobisher, 45687 Neptune, 45728 Defiance, 45729 Furious
'Royal Scot' 4-6-0:	46107 Argyll and Sutherland Highlander
'Princess Coronation' 4-6-2:	46224 Princess Alexandra, 46230 Duchess of Buccleuch
Class '2' 2-6-0:	46432
'3F' 0-6-0T:	47332, 47358, 47432, 47471, 47667, 47669
'8F' 2-8-0:	48158, 48758
'3F' 0-6-0:	57568, 57602
'3F' 0-6-0:	57653
'Clan' 4-6-2:	72005 Clan MacGregor, 72006 Clan McKenzie, 72007 Clan Mackintosh, 72008 Clan Macleod, 72009 Clan Stewart
Standard '5' 4-6-0:	73057, 73059, 73154
Standard '4' 2-6-4T:	80020
'Austerity' 2-8-0:	90595, 90763
Diesels:	D59, D63, D91, D138, D3171, D3567 D4107, D8071, D8073

Carlisle (Upperby)

Saturday 30 September 1961

Class '4' 2-6-4T:	42357, 42393, 42571
Class '4' 2-6-0:	43000
'4F' 0-6-0:	44060, 44345, 44346, 44594
'Black 5' 4-6-0:	44834, 44838, 44855, 44939, 45106, 45111, 45185, 45249, 45282, 45293, 45323, 45351, 45371, 45391, 45397, 45408, 45413, 45434, 45440
'Patriot' 4-6-0:	45510 , 45512 Bunsen, 45518 Bradshaw, 45531 Sir Frederick Harrison, 45544
'Jubilee' 4-6-0:	45588 Kashmir, 45632 Tonga, 45652 Hawke, 45728 Defiance
'Princess Coronation' 4-6-2:	46230 Duchess of Buccleuch, 46240 City of Coventry, 46249 City of Sheffield
Class '2' 2-6-0:	46433, 46457, 46458, 46489
'3F' 0-6-0T:	47269, 47288, 47292, 47295, 47326, 47614
'8F' 2-8-0:	48152. 48306, 48433, 48667
'Britannia' 4-6-2:	70017 Arrow, 70046 Anzac

Crewe South

15 March 1953

Class '4' 2-6-4T:	42113, 42571, 42617
'Crab' 2-6-0:	42783, 42856, 42920
Stanier 2-6-0:	42956, 42968
'3F' 0-6-0:	43207, 43330
'4F' 0-6-0:	44063, 44450, 44508, 44600
'Black 5' 4-6-0:	44709, 44716, 44832, 44838, 44863, 45002, 45024, 45051, 45067, 45074, 45131, 45163, 45164, 45248, 45294, 45350, 45351, 45392, 45418, 45442, 45448, 45451
'Patriot' 4-6-0:	45505 The Royal Army Ordnance Corps
'Royal Scot' 4-6-0:	46115 Scots Guardsman
Sentinel 0-4-0T:	47183, 47184
'3F' 0-6-0T:	47266, 47280, 47338, 47384, 47414, 47523, 47524, 47526, 47602, 47616, 47662, 47680
'8F' 2-8-0:	48265, 48288, 48294, 48347, 48470, 48524, 48633, 48725
'7F' 0-8-0:	48952, 49021, 49028, 49157, 49230, 49243, 49311, 49342, 49439
'0F' 0-4-0ST:	51204
'2F' 0-6-0ST:	58221
'Britannia' 4-6-2:	70025 Western Star
Standard '5' 4-6-0:	73024
Standard '4' 4-6-0:	75003, 75010

| 'Austerity' 2-8-0: | 90187, 90563, 90641, 90684, 90720, |
| Diesels: | 12000, 12001, 12002, 12035, 12036, 12050, 12051, 12052, 12053, 12078, 1831 |

Dalry Road (Edinburgh)

31 January 1965

'Black 5' 4-6-0:	44820, 45053, 45127, 45469
'B1' 4-6-0:	61245 *Murray of Elibank*
'J38' 0-6-0:	65912

20 March 1965

Class '4' 2-6-4T:	42283
'Black 5' 4-6-0:	45477, 45483
'B1' 4-6-0:	61134, 61245 *Murray of Elibank*, 61307
Standard '5' 4-6-0:	73150

2 May 1965

Class '4' 2-6-4T:	42273, 42128
'Black 5' 4-6-0:	44702, 45053, 45359, 45469
'B1' 4-6-0:	61245 *Murray of Elibank*

Haymarket (Edinburgh)

Wednesday 12 September 1956, 9.25

'Black 5' 4-6-0:	44954
'A4' 4-6-2:	60004 *William Whitelaw*, 60012 *Commonwealth of Australia*
'A3' 4-6-2:	60037 *Hyperion*, 60043 *Brown Jack*, 60068 *Sir Visto*, 60079 *Bayardo*, 60087 *Blenheim*, 60095 *Flamingo*, 60097 *Humorist*, 60101 *Cicero*
'V2' 2-6-2:	60816, 60910, 60945, 60951, 60952
'D11' 4-4-0:	62683 *Hobbie Elliott*, 62685

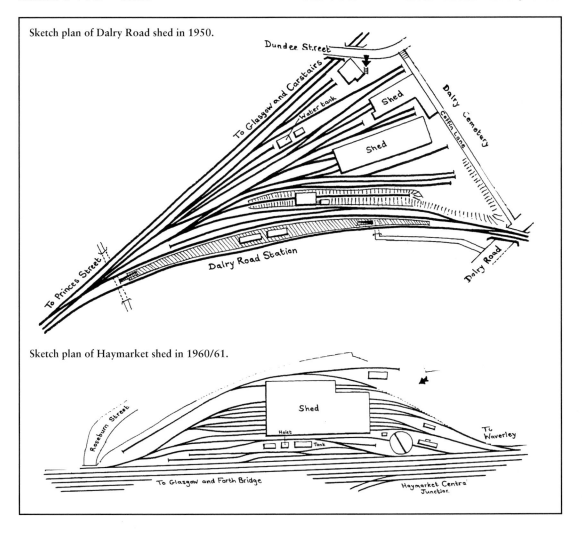

Sketch plan of Dalry Road shed in 1950.

Sketch plan of Haymarket shed in 1960/61.

Malcolm Graeme, 62691 *Laird of Balmawhapple*, 62693 *Roderick Dhu*

'D49' 4-40:	62704 *Stirlingshire*, 62705 *Lanarkshire*
'J37' 0-6-0:	64820
'J39' 0-6-0:	65258
'J38' 0-6-0:	65914
'V3' 2-6-2T:	67620, 67669
'J83' 0-6-0T:	68457, 68460

Leicester (Midland)

25 August 1963

Class '2' 2-6-2T:	41228, 41279
Class '4' 2-6-4T:	42087, 42184, 42279, 42453
Class '4' 2-6-0:	43012
'4F' 0-6-0:	43988, 44030, 44231, 44284, 44403
'Black 5' 4-6-0:	44804, 44811, 44888, 45040, 45200, 45253, 45267, 45333, 45442
'Jubilee' 4-6-0:	45556 *Nova Scotia*
'8F' 2-8-0:	48119
'B1' 4-6-0:	61249 *FitzHerbert Wright*
Standard '4' 4-6-0:	75051
Standard '2' 2-6-2T:	84029
'9F' 2-10-0:	92010, 92070, 92107, 92111, 92112, 92120, 92122, 92123
Diesels:	D3786, D3788, D3789, D3790, D3791, D5814

Old Oak Common

23 July 1962

'County' 4-6-0:	1007 *County of Brecknock*, 1009 *County of Carmarthen*, 1007 *County of Caernarvon*
'1500' 0-6-0PT:	1500, 1503, 1504, 1506
'5700' 0-6-0PT:	3754, 8757, 8761, 8771, 9658, 9704, 9706, 9707, 9709, 9710, 9784
'4700' 2-8-0:	4701, 4707, 4708
'Hall' 4-6-0:	4914 *Cranmore Hall*, 4951 *Pendeford Hall*, 4970 *Sketty Hall*, 4982 *Acton Hall*, 4983 *Albert Hall*, 5904 *Kelham Hall*, 5923 *Colston Hall*, 5932 *Haydon Hall*, 5964 *Wolseley Hall*, 5967 *Bickmarsh Hall*, 5979 *Cruckton Hall*, 5982 *Harrington Hall*, 6911 *Holker Hall*, 6920 *Barningham Hall*, 6936 *Breccles Hall*, 6942 *Eshton Hall*
'Castle' 4-6-0:	5014 *Goodrich Castle*, 5015 *Kingswear Castle*, 5032 *Usk Castle*, 5035 *Coity Castle*, 5041 *Tiverton Castle*, 5046 *Earl Cawdor*, 5052 *Earl of Radnor*, 5055 *Earl of Eldon*,

5060 *Earl of Berkeley*, 5066 *Sir Felix Pole*, 5068 *Beverston Castle*, 5080 *Defiant*, 5082 *Swordfish*, 5084 *Reading Abbey*, 5088 *Llanthony Abbey*, 7008 *Swansea Castle*, 7017 *G. J. Churchward*, 7020 *Gloucester Castle*, 7032 *Denbigh Castle*

'King' 4-6-0:	6000 *King George V*, 6009 *King Charles II*, 6010 *King Charles I*, 6016 *King Edward V*, 6021 *King Richard II*, 6025 *King Henry III*, 6026 *King John*, 6028 *King George VI*, 6029 *King Edward VIII*
'6100' 2-6-2T:	6125, 6141, 6169
'Modified Hall' 4-6-0:	6961 *Stedham Hall*, 6962 *Soughton Hall*, 6973 *Bricklehampton Hall*, 6989 *Wightwick Hall*, 6998 *Burton Agnes Hall*, 7904 *Fountains Hall*, 7906 *Fron Hall*, 7909 *Heveningham Hall*
'9400' 0-6-0PT:	8420, 8458, 9407, 9410, 9420
Standard '4' 2-6-4T:	80069, 80072, 80080, 80096, 80100, 80131, 80134
'9F' 2-10-0:	92203, 92217, 92226
Diesels:	D838 *Rapid*, D3031, D4000, D7024, D7035

Penzance

15 April 1962

'County' 4-6-0:	1004 *County of Somerset*, 1008 *County of Cardigan*
'5700' 0-6-0PT:	3635, 9748
'4500' 2-6-2T:	4564, 4670, 5508, 5537, 5562
'Castle' 4-6-0:	5003 *Lulworth Castle*
'Grange' 4-6-0:	6800 *Arlington Grange*, 6808 *Beanham Grange*, 6814 *Enborne Grange*, 6824 *Ashley Grange*, 6826 *Nannerth Grange*, 6833 *Calcot Grange*, 6835 *Eastham Grange*, 6868 *Penrhos Grange*
'9400' 0-6-0PT:	9475
Diesels:	D808 *Centaur*, D815 *Druid*, D822 *Hercules*, D849 *Superb*, D852 *Tenacious*, D859 *Vanquisher*, D6309, D6338

Perth

21 May 1961, 18.45

4F 0-6-0:	44254, 44257, 44314, 44328
'Black 5' 4-6-0:	44698, 44699, 44704, 44720, 44721, 44722, 44796, 44797, 44799, 44801, 44879, 44921, 44925, 44960, 44978, 44979, 44999, 45133, 45361, 45365, 45463, 45466, 45475, 45476, 45487, 45492

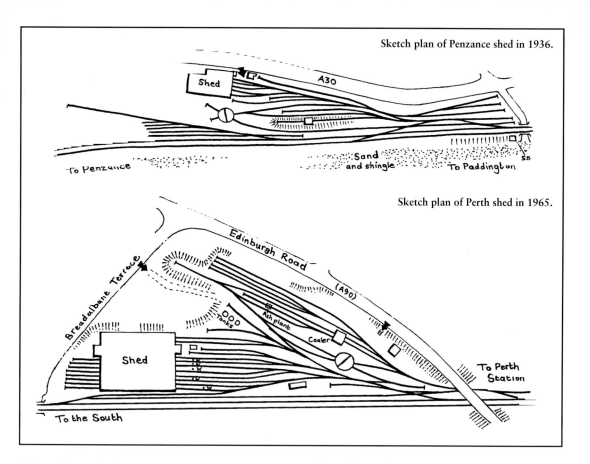

Sketch plan of Penzance shed in 1936.

Sketch plan of Perth shed in 1965.

'Princess Coronation' 4-6-2:	46231 *Duchess of Atholl*, 46237 *City of Bristol*, 46244 *King George VI*, 46252 *City of Leicester*
Class '2' 2-6-0:	46468
'3P' 4-4-0:	54486, 54500
'2P' 0-4-4T:	55173, 55217, 55233
'3F' 0-6-0:	56347
'2F' 0-6-0:	57441
'3F' 0-6-0:	57667, 57679
'V2' 2-6-2:	60888, 60959, 60970, 60973
'B1' 4-6-0:	61134
'D11' 4-4-0:	62671 *Bailie MacWheeble*
'J37' 0-6-0:	64617
'J38' 0-6-0:	65912
Standard '5' 4-6-0:	73008, 73079, 73106, 73107, 73120
Standard '4' 2-6-4T:	80126
Diesels:	D335, D3535, D3541, D3542, D3543, D3544, D3545, D5118, D5132, D5325, D5328, D5331, D5337, D5340, D5346, D6120, D6122, D6124, D6128

Polmadie (Glasgow)

10 June 1962

Class '4' 2-6-4T:	42055, 42056, 42057, 42058, 42059, 42143, 42144, 42171, 42216, 42243, 42244, 42263, 42265, 42268, 42274, 42276, 42277, 42691
'Crab' 2-6-0:	42850, 42883
'4F' 0-6-0:	44011, 44251, 44283, 44318
'Black 5' 4-6-0:	44719, 44783, 44790, 44885, 44898, 44900, 44973, 44974, 45083, 45151, 45172, 45243, 45458, 45459, 45465, 45478
'Jubilee' 4-6-0:	45583 *Assam*, 45698 *Mars*, 45719 *Glorious*, 45723 *Fearless*
'Royal Scot' 4-6-0:	46102 *Black Watch*, 46104 *Scottish Borderer*, 46114 *Coldstream Guardsman*, 46121 *Highland Light Infantry, City of Glasgow Regiment*, 46139 *The Welch Regiment*
'Princess Royal' 4-6-2:	46203 *Princess Margaret Rose*
'Princess Coronation' 4-6-2:	46221 *Queen Elizabeth*, 46223 *Princess Alice*, 46224 *Princess*

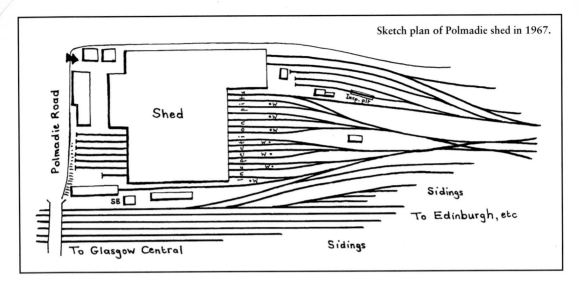

Sketch plan of Polmadie shed in 1967.

	Alexandra, 46231 Duchess of Atholl
'8F' 2-8-0:	48773, 48775, 48774
'3P' 4-4-0:	54463, 54465, 54502
'2F' 0-6-0:	57296, 57360
'3F' 0-6-0:	57555, 57581, 57620, 57622, 57625
'3F' 0-6-0:	57667, 57672, 57674, 57684
'Britannia' 4-6-2:	70023 Venus
'Clan' 4-6-2:	72000 Clan Buchanan, 72001 Clan Cameron, 72002 Clan Campbell, 72003 Clan Fraser
Standard '5' 4-6-0:	73056, 73060, 73063, 73075, 73076, 73098
Standard '3' 2-6-0:	77007, 77008, 77009
Standard '4' 2-6-4T :	80003, 80005, 80026, 80027, 80055, 80056, 80086, 80106, 80107, 80108, 80110, 80112, 80115, 80124, 80129, 80130
'Austerity' 2-8-0:	90039, 90234, 90326, 90387, 90596, 90640
Diesels:	D114, D152, D276, D311, D322, D324, D331, D341, D2431, D2432, D2433, D3199, D3383, D3529, D3906, D3908, D3910, D3911, D3913, D3916, D3917, D3918, D5093, D8086, D8119, D8120, D8124

'A2' 4-6-2:	60534 Irish Elegance, 60537 Bachelor's Button, 60538 Velocity
'V2' 2-6-2:	60813, 60816, 60836, 60840, 60873 Coldstreamer, 60883, 60892, 60894, 60910, 60931, 60933, 60937, 60951, 60965, 60969, 60971, 60973
'B1' 4-6-0:	61007 Klipspringer, 61108, 61117, 61294, 61307, 61341, 61344, 61349, 61350, 61356, 61357, 61398
'K3' 2-6-0:	61968
'J35' 0-6-0:	64510, 64519, 64527
'J37' 0-6-0:	64547, 64557, 64562, 64572, 64576, 64577, 64582, 64591, 64594, 64606, 64607, 64608, 64637
'J36' 0-6-0:	65224 Mons, 65344
'J38' 0-6-0:	65914, 65918, 65920, 65927, 65934
'V1/3' 2-6-2T:	67668
'Y9' 0-4-0 ST:	68095
'J83' 0-6-0T:	68477
'N15' 0-6-2T:	69219
Standard '4' 2-6-4T:	80003, 80022, 80026, 80055
Diesels:	D2706, D2720, D2722, D2728, D2729, D2731, D2745, D2779, D3558, D3742, D3878, D3880, D3886

St Margarets (Edinburgh)

24 August 1962

'Black 5' 4-6-0:	45161, 45178
Class '2' 2-6-0:	46462
'A4' 4-6-2:	60001 Sir Ronald Matthews
'A3' 4-6-2:	60041 Salmon Trout, 60043 Brown Jack, 60071 Tranquil, 60072 Sunstar, 60087 Blenheim

Willesden

24 July 62

Fowler 2-6-2T:	40006, 40049
Stanier 2-6-2T:	40080, 40128, 40144, 40157, 40201
Fairburn 2-6-4T:	42101, 42117, 42218, 42234
Fowler 2-6-4T:	42367

THE STEAM LOCOMOTIVE SHED

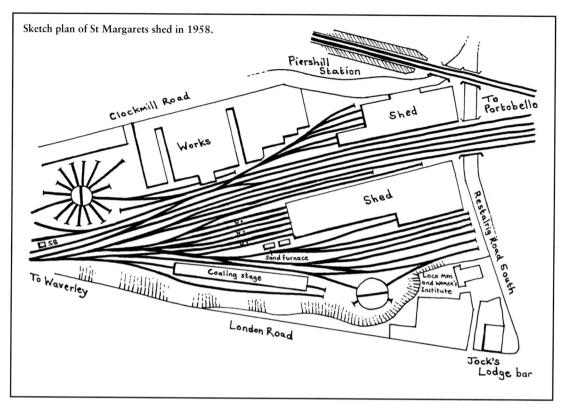

Sketch plan of St Margarets shed in 1958.

Stanier 2-6-4T:	42470, 42478, 42562, 42576, 42577, 42588, 42604, 42611, 42616		48518, 48538, 48600, 48601, 48624, 48637, 48751
Stanier 2-6-0:	42983	'7F' 0-8-0:	49413
'4F' 0-6-0:	44442	'Britannia' 4-6-2:	70021 *Morning Star*, 70025
'Black 5' 4-6-0:	45048, 45111, 45236, 45255, 45271, 45287, 45 328		*Western Star*, 70031 *Byron*, 70033 *Charles Dickens*, 70040 *Clive of India*
'Patriot' 4-6-0:	45523 *Bangor*, 45529 *Stephenson*	Standard '5' 4-6-0:	73013, 73014, 73039, 73126
'Jubilee' 4-6-0:	45555 *Quebec*, 45655 *Keith*, 45732 *Sanspareil*	Standard '4' 4-6-0:	75030, 75037, 75038, 75052, 75054
'Royal Scot' 4-6-0:	46111 *Royal Fusilier*, 46119 *Lancashire Fusilier*, 46144 *Honorable Artillery Company*, 46146 *The Rifle Brigade*, 46154 *The Hussar*	Standard '4' 2-6-0:	76023
		'9F' 2-10-0:	92086
		Diesels:	D5000, D5001, D5016, D5024, D5029, D5030, D5035, D5073, D5074, D5076, D5082, D5136, D5137, D5141, D5143, D5144, D5145, D5146, D5604, D8003, D8036, D8041, 10000
Class '2' 2-6-0:	46426, 46470		
'3F' 0-6-0T:	47302, 47304, 47307		
'8F' 2-8-0:	48036, 48325, 48368, 48449,		

SELECTED SHED VISIT LOGS

INDEX

Page numbers in **bold** refer to shed logs. (p) indicates a shed layout plan.